Oishisou!!

おいしそう!!

THE ULTIMATE ANIME DESSERT COOKBOOK

Oishisou!!

おいしそう!!

THE ULTIMATE ANIME DESSERT COOKBOOK

BY HADLEY SUI

PHOTOGRAPHY BY
EMILY HAWKES

ILLUSTRATIONS BY
MONIQUE NARBONETA ZOSA

TITAN
BOOKS
LONDON

CONTENTS

From the Panya

From the Dagashiya

Ie Ni: At Home

Issho Ni: To Share

To my host families in Yoshikawa, who were kind enough to bring me into their homes and into their lives as a daughter.

This book is intended to serve as an introduction to Japanese pastries as well as the many anime series that feature them. It is my hope that these recipes will expand your kitchen's boundaries and inspire you to explore even more of Japan's unique culinary traditions. Enjoy your impending confectionery adventures! *Itadakimasu!*

—HADLEY SUI

INTRODUCTION: A FEAST FOR THE EYES

For many of its fans, Japanese animation, or anime, is a gateway into Japanese culture, and it can fuel a lifelong passion for studying the Japanese language and all facets of the nation's daily life. Food is another entry point into this fascination with learning about Japan's culture and beliefs. As foreign anime viewers, we are transported to our very own *isekai* (or parallel universe) full of exquisite foods that are often grounded in real traditions. These foods reveal the possibilities of new flavors and experiences that are waiting for us if we allow ourselves to get lost in a new way of thinking.

Pastry in particular is one of Japan's most versatile art forms. The country's pastries have the ability to capture the ever-changing beauty of the seasons and underline the transitory aspect of our experience of the world. Japanese pastries have ties to the traditional art of the tea ceremony (*sadō*, or "way of tea"), but they are also influenced by various foreign cultures while maintaining their own unique ethos.

The recipes in this book are rooted in my research of traditional and nontraditional pastry, highlighted by anime and the role it plays in its native land. While living in Japan, I had the good fortune to be able to attend Japanese confectionary classes at Kyoto pastry institutions such as Kameya Yoshinaga, where I formed an appreciation for the process of pastry creation as well as a desire to share the art form with others. To reflect the fantastical nature of anime, some of the recipes in this volume draw upon nontraditional colors and forms; in these cases, their original appearance and context are noted.

Oishisou!! The Ultimate Anime Dessert Cookbook is a tribute to the expertise and creativity of Japan's anime creators and its pastry chefs, written from the perspective of a mesmerized and hungry outsider looking in at their wonderfully sweet and addicting creations. Use these recipes as a launching point for creating the sweets seen in your favorite anime and exploring their connection to modern Japan.

JAPANESE PASTRY BASICS
THE ORIGINS OF JAPANESE PASTRY

Japanese pastries tend to fall into two categories: *wagashi* and *yougashi*. The word *kashi* indicates "confections," and originally referred to nuts and fruits. It is the basis for both of these terms. *Wagashi* are traditional Japanese sweets ("wa" indicates "Japanese"). The evolution of *wagashi* was influenced by the rise of the tea ceremony in Japan, as well as the Chinese tradition of dim sum. Japan's very first *wagashi* are speculated to have been *dango*, or small ball-shaped sweets. They were most likely originated by people supplementing their diet with acorns due to an insufficient food supply. Raw acorns are too bitter to eat, so they were ground and soaked in water to lessen their bitterness, then cooked into spherical shapes. *Dango* have become a mainstay in Japan's *wagashi* scene, though they are now typically made with rice flour and bean paste rather than acorns.

During the Nara period (710–794 AD), ambassadors brought Chinese culture to Japan. It was at this time that deep-fried and boiled dumpling-style confections were introduced to Japan, though they were initially used primarily for offerings at shrines and temples. In addition to *dango* and dumplings, a third predecessor of *wagashi* was *tenshin*, a word derived from a Japanese Zen Buddhist term that means "little things to add to the empty stomach." Monks consumed these foods, which included soups, dumplings, and noodles, to tide themselves over between meditation sessions. Because of their Buddhist origins, these foods were vegetarian, and they became today's *yōkan* and *manju*. Today, *wagashi* are unique in their devotion to seasonality, often being influenced in both form and flavor by the subtleties of each season in Japan. Their designs and ingredients also draw inspiration from poetry, old and new, as well as pop culture.

Yougashi refers to Western-style sweets, such as cakes, which are often made with ingredients like white sugar and eggs. The popular strawberry shortcakes, crêpes, and Swiss roll cakes are all considered to be *yougashi*. Nowadays, these treats are prevalent in Japan, with many shops specializing in cakes, breads, and more. Japanese ingredients and flavors are often incorporated into *yougashi* confections, such as breads made with *mochiko* rice flour and cakes flavored with matcha.

Nanbangashi, another term in Japan's pastry taxonomy, are confections adopted from Portugal and Spain during the Muromachi period (1336–1573 AD), when missionaries came to Japan to facilitate trade and promote Christianity. A type of *nanbangashi* that is still popular is *konpeito,* a small crystal candy made from sugar instead of natural sweeteners like *amazura* (ivy sap) that were commonly used when *wagashi* were first introduced. Unlike the majority of previous *wagashi* types that were meant for the elite, *nanbangashi* were consumed by the general public.

In addition to displaying a keen attention to seasonality, Japanese pastries tend to reflect a sharp awareness and celebration of local flavors. Japan's *omiyage* gifting culture revolves around hyper-local produce, flavors, and artisanal specialties. It is common to bring boxes of *omiyage* souvenir snacks back to family and friends after traveling. The country's variety of terrains and climates allows for a wide range of produce to flourish, and its long tradition of artisan crafts has helped to elevate each regional specialty to its highest form. Many of the pastry varieties in this book have been adapted in Japan to reflect local flavors and heritage.

THE JAPANESE PASTRY PANTRY

Here are a few of the Japanese specialty pastry ingredients used in this book. These can be sourced at Japanese supermarkets such as Mitsuwa and at the Korean-American chain H Mart, or through online stores like Bokksu Grocery.

Anko
Anko, or adzuki bean paste, is made from boiling, crushing, and sweetening red adzuki beans. It is frequently used in Japanese pastries and can be purchased premade at Japanese grocery stores if you don't have time to make it yourself. *Koshi an* and *tsubu an* are types of *anko*.

Joshinko
Joshinko is a flour made from nonglutinous short-grain rice. It can result in chewier textures than *shiratamako*.

Kabocha
Kabocha is a Japanese winter squash with a bright yellow-orange interior, similar in taste to an acorn squash. When "pumpkin" is called out as a flavor in Japan, it usually means kabocha.

Kanten
Similar to agar (also called agar-agar), kanten is a gelatinous substance made from red algae that is found in many Japanese pastries. It usually comes in flaked or powdered form and is used as a vegetarian alternative to gelatin. It is semitranslucent and is considered different from agar because it comes from a different species of algae.

Kinako
Kinako is soybean powder, often used as a topping on mochi pastries.

Koshi an
Koshi an is the smooth, strained variety of red bean paste.

Kurozato
Kurozato is Japanese black sugar, an unrefined cane sugar that becomes a dark molasses when heated. It is often produced in Okinawa.

Matcha
Matcha is powdered green tea, one of the most common flavors in Japanese desserts. It has a bitter, earthy flavor and is often paired with *wagashi* during the Japanese tea ceremony. Matcha is available in different grades: ceremonial, premium, and culinary. While culinary is the cheapest and most common grade, it has a duller green color and browns when baking, so I recommend premium grade matcha for the recipes in this book. (Japanese brands like Ippodo Tea and Maeda-en are good sources for premium matcha.)

Mirin
Mirin is a Japanese rice wine used only for cooking. It contains more sugar and less alcohol than sake.

Miso
Miso is fermented soybean paste and comes in red, yellow, and white varieties. Red miso is fermented the longest and has the strongest flavor.

Mochigome
Mochigome is glutinous (sticky) rice, used for making *mochiko*.

Mochiko
Mochiko is cooked, glutinous sweet rice flour. It is traditionally combined and cooked with water and sugar to make mochi.

Potato starch
Potato starch has similar thickening qualities to cornstarch and can also be used to dust your work surface when making sticky confections.

Satsumaimo
Satsumaimo is the Japanese word for sweet potato and refers to the Japanese variety with a red skin and yellow or white interior.

Sesame seeds
Both black and white sesame seeds are common ingredients and toppings in Japanese pastry. Toasted sesame seeds can be ground into a paste, which releases their signature nutty flavor.

Shiratamako
Shiratamako is a glutinous rice flour that yields a more durable and elastic dough than *mochiko*, which makes it great as an outer layer on *wagashi*. It is made from uncooked glutinous rice that is washed, soaked, ground, pressed, and finally dried into large granules.

Silken tofu
Silken tofu is a variety of tofu that has the firmness and consistency of custard. It is used in baking to achieve a chewy texture.

Tsubu an
Tsubu an is coarse red bean paste that has chunks of adzuki red beans still intact within it.

Warabi mochiko
Warabi *mochiko* is a flour made from the starch of the bracken (fern) root, which gives certain pastries their jellylike texture, distinct from the texture produced by *mochiko*.

THE WORLD OF JAPANESE PASTRIES

This book is organized into six sections, each covering a category of locations where pastries are enjoyed both in anime and in Japan itself. These are *matsuri* (festivals), *konbini* (convenience stores), *panya* (bakeries), *dagashiya* (candy stores), *ie ni* (at home), and *issho ni* (to share). There is a lot of overlap between these settings; certain styles of treats are sold at a variety of different sites. Japan's dessert culture is boundless, and this book should serve as an appetizer for further exploration!

Matsuri: Festivals

Also called *omatsuri*, festivals are abundant in Japan. Some of the most common are summer festivals (*natsu matsuri*), cherry blossom festivals (*sakura matsuri*), and school/culture festivals (*bunkasai* or *gakuensai*). Bunkasai festivals often involve students running their own stalls and activities. Festival treats range from refreshing *kakigori* to the universally beloved cotton candy.

AS SEEN IN: *Lucky Star; The Quintessential Quintuplets; Barakamon*

Konbini: Convenience Stores

Japan's dazzling devotion to its convenience stores—popular chains include FamilyMart, 7-Eleven, and Lawson—has been gaining attention in the West. These establishments are wonderlands of packaged snack foods, breads, and chilled pastries such as *purin* as well as a plethora of sweets, and many sell a variety of full bento meals. You'll be sure to find everything you need and much more at a Japanese convenience store!

AS SEEN IN: *Convenience Store Boy Friends; Sound! Euphonium; A Certain Scientific Railgun*

Panya: Bakeries

Bakeries in Japan are often French-influenced and feature a wide range of snack breads as well as artisanal loaves. Here you will find the fresh-baked versions of the breads sold in convenience stores, such as melon *pan* and cream puffs. *Panya* almost always sell *shokupan*, a thick-cut fluffy white milk bread, which is the most common variety of loaf bread in Japan.

AS SEEN IN: *Yakitate!! Japan; Yumeiro Patissiere; Antique Bakery*

Dagashiya: Candy Stores

Dagashiya shops grew popular during the Meiji period (1868–1912 AD), though the oldest one, Kamikawaguchiya, was founded in 1781. *Dagashi* refers to cheap candy and snacks; the treats sold at a *dagashiya* usually cost no more than 50 yen, or around 50 cents. *Dagashiya* tend to carry candy, rice crackers, and small cakes, often historically made with corn syrup rather than the more expensive white sugar.

AS SEEN IN: *Fushigi Dagashiya Zenitendō; Non Non Biyori; Himouto! Umaru-chan*

Ie Ni: At Home

Japanese treats are frequently made at home, or the *ie*. Many Japanese homes, however, are not equipped with large ovens for baking. The majority of recipes in this section are therefore either steamed or simply don't require an oven.

AS SEEN IN: *Anohana: The Flower We Saw That Day; Cardcaptor Sakura: Clear Card; Encouragement of Climb*

Issho Ni: To Share

The Japanese phrase *ichigo ichie* translates to "one time, one meeting." In essence, this is a reminder to appreciate every experience as it happens, because all moments in time are unique and fleeting. It is derived from the Japanese tea ceremony, which represents purity, tranquility, respect, and harmony—all elements that can be incorporated into our daily lives. The recipes in this section are all best when shared with someone special.

AS SEEN IN: *Erased; Tamako Market; March Comes in Like a Lion*

FOOD TROPES IN ANIME

Desserts are everywhere in anime, but they most often appear in specific story contexts that have become common narrative touchstones throughout the genre. Be on the lookout for these tropes as you watch your favorite series!

Toast of Tardiness

In shojo anime, there is often a scene in which the heroine runs out of her house, late for school or a different appointment, with a piece of breakfast toast hanging out of her mouth. This is a common way to start an episode.

AS SEEN IN: *K-On!!; Nisekoi; Code Geass*

Valentine's Day Chocolate

Valentine's Day in Japan is often marked by making chocolates and giving them to the special boy in your life, or to a senpai (upperclassman) in admiration. Many slice-of-life anime series feature high schoolers making these treats in secret and working up the courage to give them to the object of their admiration.

AS SEEN IN: *From Me to You; The Pet Girl of Sakurasou; You and Me*

The Christmas Party

Christmas in Japan is typically celebrated with friends instead of family. In anime, a Christmas party where characters gather around a Christmas cake often occurs toward the end of the season, immediately preceding a culminating event for the main character.

AS SEEN IN: *Toradora!; My Hero Academia; Himouto! Umaru-chan; The Disappearance of Haruhi Suzumiya*

The School Festival

School festival episodes in anime are always filled with commotion and excitement. Students work together to create engaging booths and experiences such as *takoyaki* stalls, maid cafés, and haunted houses, and the festivals are open to prospective students as well as anyone else who wants to attend.

AS SEEN IN: *My Hero Academia; K-On!!; My Teen Romantic Comedy SNAFU*

The Summer Festival

Summer festivals often feature a variety of Japanese foods such as *yakisoba* and *kakigori*, as well as traditional festival games such as catching goldfish with a paper net that disintegrates when it gets too waterlogged (*kingyo-sukui*).

AS SEEN IN: *The Quintessential Quintuplets; Noragami; Pretty Cure*

The Trip to the Beach

Many anime have a summer vacation episode in which characters spend a sunny day bonding at the beach. It is a break from more intense plotlines and usually includes a beach barbecue or soft-serve ice cream.

AS SEEN IN: *DARLING in the FRANXX; Love, Chunibyo & Other Delusions; Gurren Lagann*

JAPANESE PASTRY STAPLE:
SWEET BEAN PASTE

Bean paste is a critical ingredient in many Japanese pastries. It is thought that Japan was introduced to bean paste in the seventh century via China and that it was originally a savory ingredient mixed with salt. The sweet version gained overwhelming popularity during the Edo period (1603–1868 AD) when sugar became more widely available, and this is now the predominant meaning of "red bean paste." Revisit these recipes as required for various fillings and toppings used throughout this book. Bean paste keeps well for 2 to 3 days in the refrigerator and can be frozen for up to 1 week.

RED BEAN PASTE

Time: 1 hour 15 minutes plus overnight soaking • **Yield:** About 2 cups

1 cup dry adzuki red beans

4 cups water

1⅓ cups sugar

¼ teaspoon salt

1. Soak the adzuki beans overnight, or for at least 6 hours. (Refrain from soaking beans for more than 24 hours to prevent them from sprouting.)

2. Rinse and drain the beans, then add to a large pot with water and bring to a boil over medium-high heat. Once the water is boiling, bring the heat down to a simmer and cook for 1 hour over low heat.

3. Drain the beans, return them to the pot, and add the sugar and salt. Cook for 8 to 10 minutes over low heat, stirring to mash the beans so that a paste begins to form.

4. Take the bean paste off the heat and transfer it to a heatproof bowl. This is now *tsubu an* (coarse red bean paste); you may want to pulse the bean paste in a food processor for 5 seconds to break up any larger remaining chunks. For *koshi an* (smooth red bean paste), strain the bean paste through a fine mesh sieve.

5. Keep refrigerated in an airtight container for up to 3 days, or freeze.

WHITE BEAN PASTE

Time: 1 hour 45 minutes plus overnight soaking • **Yield:** About 2 cups

1 cup large dry white beans (butter beans or cannellini beans)

4 cups water

1 1/3 cups sugar

1/4 teaspoon salt

1. Soak the white beans overnight, or for at least 6 hours. (Refrain from soaking beans for more than 24 hours to prevent them from sprouting.)

2. Rinse and drain the beans. Remove bean skins by hand, then add the beans to a large pot with water and bring to a boil over medium heat. Once the water is boiling, bring the heat down to a simmer and cook for 1 hour over low heat.

3. Drain the beans, return them to the pot, and add the sugar and salt. Cook for 15 minutes over low heat, stirring to mash the beans so that a paste begins to form.

4. Take the bean paste off the heat and transfer to a heatproof bowl, then pulse the bean paste in a food processor for 30 seconds, or until smooth.

5. Keep refrigerated in an airtight container for up to 3 days, or freeze.

FROM THE
MATSURI

氷

CHOCO BANANA

Time: 10 minutes plus 15 minutes freezing • **Yield:** 6 frozen banana pops

It's easy to see why this food stall snack would be a favorite on hot summer days. Who wouldn't crave a frozen banana coated in a luscious chocolate shell and sprinkled with a decorative topping? For this recipe, I recommend topping with crumbled Pocky candy, your favorite cereal, or healthier toppings like chopped walnuts or almond slivers.

3 ripe bananas

2 cups high quality chocolate, chopped

½ cup topping of your choice

6 popsicle sticks or skewers

1. Cover the bottom of a small sheet pan with a piece of wax paper. Make sure the pan can fit into your freezer.

2. Peel bananas and cut them in half crosswise. Without splitting the sides of the fruit, insert a popsicle stick into the base of each banana piece.

3. In a medium microwave-safe bowl, heat chocolate in a microwave on medium setting for 30 seconds and stir. Continue heating in 30-second increments and stirring until the chocolate is completely melted.

4. Dunk each banana pop into the melted chocolate, using a spoon to make sure the entire surface of the banana is covered, and lay each banana pop onto the wax paper in your pan.

5. Immediately sprinkle with your choice of topping, then freeze for at least 15 minutes before eating.

AS SEEN IN: *Isekai Quartet; Gourmet Girl Graffiti; Remake Our Life!*

In *Isekai Quartet*, a motley group of characters from four different fantasy worlds find themselves in a new dimension and forced to attend the same school. Upon learning that they need to prepare for a school festival the following week requiring the creation of both a food stall and a play, Viktoriya Serebryakov (originally from *Youjo Senki: Saga of Tanya the Evil*) is moved to proclaim, "CHOCO BANANA!"—evidently her favorite festival treat.

KAKIGORI

Kakigori is a popular dish at summer festivals in Japan, and there are also specialty cafés devoted to making it. *Kakigori* was invented sometime around the eleventh century as a treat for the wealthy, because it required large blocks of ice to be cut in the winter and carefully kept in storehouses at great expense until summertime. This original *kakigori* was shaved by hand with a knife and was flavored with *amazura* (ivy sap). The modern *kakigori* has a smoother and fluffier consistency than a snow cone, thanks to the method by which the ice is shaved. I recommend using a small *kakigori* machine to make these recipes, but if you don't have access to one, the ice can be crushed in a blender.

AS SEEN IN: *Non Non Biyori; Dropkick on My Devil!; Urusei Yatsura*

Early in *Non Non Biyori*, Hotaru spends the day with her senpai, Komari. In an effort to seem more mature, Hotaru (with some help from her mom) puts together an outfit that is so chic that Komari mistakes her for a stylish adult from out of town. During their outing, Hotaru orders them both glittering matcha *kakigori* shaved ice in hopes of impressing Komari even more, given that it is considered a "grown-up" flavor. The following recipes contain plenty of sweet simple syrup, so any age and palate can enjoy these refreshing delights!

MATCHA MAGIC KAKIGORI

Time: 15 minutes • **Yield:** 1 bowl

MATCHA WHIPPED CREAM

½ cup heavy cream

2 teaspoons matcha powder, sifted

1 teaspoon honey

KAKIGORI

2 cups ice

2 tablespoons matcha powder, dissolved
   in ¼ cup water

3 tablespoons simple syrup

½ cup sweetened condensed milk

1 teaspoon matcha powder for garnishing

1 pinch edible silver glitter for garnishing

TO MAKE THE WHIPPED CREAM:

1. In a cold mixing bowl, whip heavy cream with a hand mixer until soft peaks form, about 3 minutes on a high speed. Add the matcha powder and the honey, and whip for 30 more seconds until combined.

TO MAKE THE KAKIGORI:

1. Prepare shaved ice according to machine instructions, and pour into a medium bowl or sundae cup.

3. Mix the matcha liquid and the simple syrup together. Pour the matcha mixture over the shaved ice, then pour the sweetened condensed milk over the ice.

4. Spoon matcha whipped cream onto the shaved ice, and garnish with the matcha powder, using a fine mesh sieve to sprinkle it over the top. Finish with a pinch of edible glitter.

ORANGE BLOSSOM KAKIGORI

Time: 15 minutes • **Yield:** 1 bowl

1 tangerine peel

2 cups ice

½ tablespoon orange blossom water

⅓ cup simple syrup

1 tangerine, peeled, segmented and frozen

1. Prepare the tangerine peel garnish: Twist the tangerine peel around a large straw and pin its ends in place. Freeze the peel while preparing the *kakigori*.

2. Prepare shaved ice according to machine instructions, and pour into a medium sundae cup or dessert dish.

3. In a small bowl, mix orange blossom water with simple syrup. Pour mixture over shaved ice to taste.

4. Arrange frozen tangerine slices around the edge of your *kakigori* dish, then unpin the frozen tangerine peel from its straw and garnish the kakigori with the peel spiral.

MINI WATAAME

Time: 40 minutes • **Yield:** 4 mini cotton candy puffs

Wataame (also called *watagashi*), or cotton candy, was introduced to Japan shortly after its invention in the United States in 1897. Today it is typically sold in bags decorated with manga and anime characters, and just like in the West, it is also a common treat at fairs and festivals. This stovetop version allows you to enjoy it at home without a cotton candy machine. Though the recipe requires patience, you'll be glad you put in the effort to experience this taste of summer and childhood.

2 cups sugar

½ cup corn syrup

½ cup water

1 pinch salt

2 drops green gel food coloring

3 drops melon extract or flavor extract of your choice

4 large lollipop sticks

AS SEEN IN: *Barakamon; Akkun to Kanojo; Higehiro*

In episode 10 of *Barakamon*, exiled calligrapher Handa Seishu has the opportunity to go to a summer festival, something he has never experienced before because of his single-minded devotion to his art. At the festival, he experiences *wataame* for the first time and orders a supersized version. Whether you're experiencing cotton candy for the first or the hundredth time, this recipe is guaranteed to put a smile on your face!

1. Clear a large work space and cover it with plastic wrap. This recipe gets messy!

2. With a pastry brush and dish of water on hand, stir the sugar, corn syrup, water, and salt together with a rubber spatula in a medium pan over medium-high heat.

3. Once the sugar has melted, stop stirring and cook the mixture until it reaches 320°F on a candy thermometer. As the sugar cooks, crystals may form on the side of your pan. Dip your pastry brush in water and dissolve them as they form.

4. Once the sugar mixture reaches 320°F, take the mixture off the heat and pour it into a separate medium bowl. Add the food coloring and flavor extract, and mix to combine. (You will have about 10 minutes to work with the sugar until it solidifies; if that happens before you are done mixing, microwave the mix for 3 to 5 minutes.)

5. Dip a whisk into the sugar mixture and drizzle the liquid onto your prepared work space in a nest pattern from a height of at least 1 foot. The strands of sugar will be thicker than those of cotton candy made with a machine, but the higher you drop the sugar from, the thinner the strands will be!

6. Form the strands into clumps around your lollipop sticks while the mixture is still warm and workable.

RINGO AME AND ICHIGO AME

Time: 30 minutes • **Yield:** 4 candy apples or 10 candy strawberries

You will almost always find a stall selling *ringo ame* (candy apples) at Japanese festivals. These are sometimes accompanied by other candied fruits, such as strawberries (*ichigo ame*) or grapes, which are smaller and easier to eat. The creation of *ringo ame* may have been influenced by China's *tanghulu*, or traditionally candied hawthorn berries, or by the candy apples that were invented in 1908 by a confectioner in Newark, New Jersey.

1½ cups water

3 cups sugar

1 teaspoon white vinegar

4 whole tart apples (such as Granny Smith) or 10 whole strawberries, hulled

4 large bamboo skewers (or disposable chopsticks) or 5 small bamboo skewers

¼ teaspoon red gel food coloring

¼ teaspoon ground cinnamon

1 pinch edible red glitter

1. In a large pot over medium heat, stir the water, sugar, and vinegar together. Once the sugar has dissolved, stop stirring and bring to a boil.

2. While waiting for your mixture to boil, line a large baking tray with wax paper. Rinse your apples or strawberries and dry them completely. Pierce each fruit with a bamboo skewer. Feel free to put two or three strawberries on each skewer.

3. Continue heating your sugar mixture for about 20 minutes, or until a candy thermometer reads 300°F. Quickly remove the pot from the heat once you reach this temperature.

4. Mix in your red food coloring and cinnamon with a rubber spatula, and wait 1 minute for bubbles to disappear. Then angle your pot so that the majority of the sugar liquid flows to one side. Quickly dip each fruit into the mixture so that it is completely coated, and place the dipped fruit on your prepared wax paper tray.

5. Garnish with edible red glitter, and let the coating cool and solidify before enjoying!

AS SEEN IN: *The Quintessential Quintuplets; Guilty Crown; Iroduku: The World in Colors*

In episode 4 of *The Quintessential Quintuplets*, Futaro Uesugi, his sister Riha, and the Nakano quintuplets go to a summer festival where they get separated in the crowds. The friends encounter many treats throughout the evening, and Riha gives Yotsuba (the fourth quintuplet) her candy apple so that Yotsuba doesn't wander from their meeting spot to get snacks.

TAIYAKI

Taiyaki are fish-shaped pancakes filled with cream or red bean paste that are sold at festivals and roadside stands. *Tai* means "sea bream," a type of fish that is supposed to bring good luck. *Taiyaki* was first sold in Japan in 1909 during the Meiji period (1868–1912 AD) as a reshaped form of *imagawayaki*, a popular circular snack composed of bean paste wrapped in a flour coating.

AS SEEN IN: *Miss Kobayashi's Dragon Maid; Kanon; Princess Jellyfish*

Early in Season 2 of *Miss Kobayashi's Dragon Maid*, Elma (a dragon in human form) is seen indulging in a bag of *taiyaki* pancakes. As she walks along, minding her own business, she is suddenly punched in the face by Tohru (also a dragon). Elma quickly finishes her *taiyaki* before explaining that she's not the culprit that Tohru is looking for. Just like Elma, I guarantee that nothing will be able to distract you from these luscious filled pancakes!

You will need a *taiyaki* mold to make these recipes. *Taiyaki* molds come in electric or stovetop varieties. If you are using an electric mold, follow the appliance's instructions. If you are cooking on your stovetop, follow the instructions below. I recommend removing any leftover bits of cooked batter from the *taiyaki* mold in between cooking each pancake. In addition to the Classic *Taiyaki* recipe, I am also including a Strawberry Banana *Taiyaki* (page 27) variant as a tribute to summery *natsu matsuri* flavors, as well as a more indulgent Red Velvet Nutella *Taiyaki* (page 28) version. Be careful to not add too much filling, or your *taiyaki* will burst at the seams!

HOMEMADE PASTRY CREAM

Time: 15 minutes plus 2 hours refrigeration • **Yield:** About 1½ cups

1 cup whole milk

1 teaspoon vanilla extract

¼ cup sugar

1½ tablespoons cornstarch

⅛ teaspoon salt

2 large egg yolks

1 tablespoon unsalted butter, cubed

1. In a large bowl, set up an ice bath for a medium saucepan.

2. In a medium saucepan, mix the milk and the vanilla extract. Bring to a simmer over medium-low heat.

3. In a medium heatproof mixing bowl, whisk together the sugar, cornstarch, salt, and yolks. Then pour in the simmering milk mixture while whisking continuously to combine.

4. Pour all of the contents back into the saucepan and continue to whisk over medium-low heat until the mixture begins to thicken, about 5 minutes.

5. Continue to whisk until large bubbles begin to form, about 1 minute. Once the mixture is bubbling, whisk for 1 additional minute, then remove from heat and place the pan in the prepared ice bath.

6. Add cubed butter and whisk to combine, then strain the pastry cream mixture through a fine mesh sieve into a medium bowl to remove any pieces of egg.

7. Cover the pastry cream with plastic wrap, making sure the plastic wrap is in contact with the cream so that a skin doesn't form on its surface while it rests, and refrigerate for at least 2 hours.

CLASSIC TAIYAKI

Time: 1 hour • **Yield**: 5 pancakes

1¼ cups cake flour

1 teaspoon baking powder

3 tablespoons light brown sugar

1 teaspoon baking soda

1 large egg

½ cup whole milk

¼ cup water

1 teaspoon soy sauce

Nonstick cooking spray or 1 tablespoon vegetable oil

5 tablespoons pastry cream (Homemade Pastry Cream, page 24) or Red Bean Paste (page 12)

1. In a large bowl, whisk together the cake flour, baking powder, light brown sugar, and baking soda.

2. In a separate medium bowl, whisk together the egg, whole milk, water, and soy sauce.

3. Pour the wet mixture into the dry mixture and stir to form a batter. Cover bowl with plastic wrap and let rest for 30 minutes.

4. Spray your *taiyaki* mold with nonstick cooking spray, or apply vegetable oil using a small piece of paper towel, being sure to reach all of the mold's nooks and crannies.

5. Spoon batter into half of your *taiyaki* mold so that all corners are filled, about 1½ tablespoons. Close the mold and cook over medium heat for 1 minute.

6. Open the mold and spoon 1 tablespoon of pastry cream or red bean paste into the cooked *taiyaki* batter. Close the mold and cook for an additional 1½ minutes.

7. Cover the pastry cream or red bean paste with more *taiyaki* batter so that the cream or paste is covered entirely.

8. Flip the mold and cook for 2 minutes on the other side. Your final *taiyaki* should be a light golden brown color.

STRAWBERRY BANANA TAIYAKI

Time: 1 hour 10 minutes • **Yield**: 5 pancakes

1¼ cups cake flour

1 teaspoon baking powder

3 tablespoons sugar

One .3-ounce pack strawberry Jell-O mix

1 teaspoon baking soda

1 large egg

¾ cup whole milk

Nonstick cooking spray or 1 tablespoon vegetable oil

1 small banana, peeled, finely chopped, and macerated with 1 teaspoon sugar

5 teaspoons strawberry jam

1. In a large bowl, whisk together the cake flour, baking powder, sugar, strawberry Jell-O mix, and baking soda.

2. In a separate medium bowl, combine the egg and the whole milk.

3. Pour the wet mixture into the dry mixture and stir to combine. Cover the bowl with plastic wrap and let rest for 30 minutes.

4. Spray your *taiyaki* mold with nonstick cooking spray, or apply vegetable oil using a small piece of paper towel, being sure to reach all of the mold's nooks and crannies.

5. Spoon batter into half of your *taiyaki* mold so that all corners are filled, about 1½ tablespoons. Close the mold and cook over medium-low heat for 1 minute.

6. Open the mold and spoon 1 tablespoon of chopped banana along with 1 teaspoon strawberry jam into the cooked *taiyaki* batter. Close the mold and cook for an additional 1½ minutes.

7. Cover the fruit with more *taiyaki* batter so that the filling is covered entirely.

8. Flip the mold and cook for 2 minutes on the other side. Your final *taiyaki* should be pink with golden brown around the edges.

RED VELVET NUTELLA TAIYAKI

Time: 1 hour • **Yield:** 5 pancakes

1¼ cups cake flour

1 teaspoon baking powder

3 tablespoons sugar

1 tablespoon cocoa powder

1 teaspoon baking soda

1 large egg

½ teaspoon red gel food coloring

¾ cup whole milk

Nonstick cooking spray or 1 tablespoon vegetable oil

5 tablespoons Nutella or Speculoos cookie butter, chilled

1. In a large bowl, whisk together the cake flour, baking powder, sugar, cocoa powder, and baking soda.

2. In a separate medium bowl, combine the egg, food coloring, and whole milk.

3. Pour the wet mixture into the dry mixture and stir to combine. Cover the bowl with plastic wrap and let rest for 30 minutes.

4. Spray your *taiyaki* mold with nonstick cooking spray, or apply vegetable oil using a small piece of paper towel, being sure to reach all of the mold's nooks and crannies.

5. Spoon batter into half of your *taiyaki* mold so that all corners are filled, about 1½ tablespoons. Close the mold and cook over medium heat for 1 minute.

6. Open the mold and spoon 1 tablespoon of Nutella into the cooked *taiyaki* batter. Close the mold and cook for an additional 1½ minutes.

7. Cover the Nutella with more *taiyaki* batter so that the Nutella is covered entirely.

8. Flip the mold and cook for 2 minutes on the other side. Your final *taiyaki* exterior will be a toasted red color.

YAKIIMO

Time: 1 hour 10 minutes • **Yield**: 5 potatoes

Sweet potato is a popular flavor in Japan, especially in autumn. *Yakiimo* are often sold from carts that play their own songs, in the same way that ice cream trucks play music in the United States. They are mouthwateringly good without any enhancement; butter and sugar aren't necessary additions, but they can be welcome. Wrapping the potatoes in foil while baking them gives them a cake-like texture, or you can bake them without a foil wrap for a crispier exterior.

5 large *satsumaimo* (Japanese sweet potatoes)
5 tablespoons salted butter or sunflower butter (optional)

1. Preheat your oven to 375°F.
2. Wash and dry the sweet potatoes.
3. Poke a few holes in the potatoes with a fork or knife, wrap them in foil, and place them on a large sheet pan, evenly spaced.
4. Bake for 1 hour, let cool for 5 to 10 minutes, and enjoy! If the result is too sweet, consider adding 1 tablespoon of butter or sunflower butter to taste.

AS SEEN IN: *Your Lie in April; Hibike Euphonium; Love Live! Sunshine!!*

Yakiimo are warm, whole roasted *satsumaimo*, Japan's iconic sweet potato with red skin and a beautiful golden or white interior. In *Your Lie in April*, Kousei Arima brings a *yakiimo* to his piano student Nagi Aiza as a peace offering to apologize for his harsh teaching style. With the delicious potato at stake, Nagi can't resist forgiving him. The next time you need to smooth things over with a friend, be sure to make them a *yakiimo* to sweeten the deal!

FROM THE
KONBINI

PURIN
JAPANESE CUSTARD PUDDING

Time: 1 hour 15 minutes plus 2 hours chilling time • **Yield:** Five 3-inch pudding cups

Custard puddings originated in Europe, but Japan has taken its appreciation for these jiggly desserts to the next level. A striking butter-yellow pudding topped with a distinct caramel sauce layer, *purin*—also known as crème caramel and flan—is ubiquitous in anime and is often sold in convenience stores, eaten at home, or even used to garnish larger shared desserts such as parfaits. This recipe is for *yaki*, or baked, pudding, but you can also make a steamed (*mushi*) version or use gelatin for a no-bake option.

PUDDING

3 cups water, or enough to surround the pudding molds with 1½ inches of water

Nonstick butter cooking spray

2 cups whole milk

⅔ cup sugar

1 teaspoon vanilla extract

4 large eggs

¼ cup fresh or macerated fruit (such as whole raspberries, halved cherries, or chopped kiwi) for garnishing

Fresh mint sprigs for garnishing

CARAMEL SAUCE

6 tablespoons sugar

3 tablespoons water

AS SEEN IN: *Assassination Classroom; The Moment You Fall in Love; Nanana's Buried Treasure*

In Season 2 of *Assassination Classroom*, Kaede Kayano and a group of her classmates create a gigantic "killer pudding" with a bomb hidden inside. Designed to be irresistible to their homeroom teacher, Koro Sensei, a sweets-loving alien who is the subject of constant assassination attempts, this monstrous confection is literally as tall as the school itself. Rather than eating his way to destruction, however, Koro Sensei disables the bomb and shares the pudding with his students.

1. To start the pudding: Preheat your oven to 300°F. At the same time, bring water to a simmer in a medium saucepan over medium heat.

2. Lightly spray five 3-inch diameter molds with nonstick butter cooking spray.

3. To make the caramel sauce: In another medium saucepan over medium-high heat, warm sugar and 2 tablespoons of water. Cook until light amber in color, about 5 minutes, then add the remaining 1 tablespoon of water and stir.

4. Evenly distribute the caramel sauce in the bottom of each pudding mold.

5. To make the pudding: In a new medium saucepan, heat the milk on medium heat to 140°F, about 3 minutes. Add the sugar and the vanilla extract and stir slowly until dissolved, then remove from heat.

6. Beat the eggs in a medium bowl, then slowly incorporate the warm milk mixture into the egg mixture while constantly whisking.

7. Strain the mixture through a fine mesh sieve to remove any cooked egg pieces, then evenly distribute the mixture in the pudding molds.

8. Fill a large baking pan with about 1½ inches of the simmering water and place the pudding molds inside, making sure that the water does not get into the molds. The water should only go halfway up the sides of your molds.

9. Bake for 1 hour, or until the pudding is no longer liquid and jiggles a bit. Refrigerate for at least 2 hours.

10. Using a knife, carefully trace the outside edge of your puddings to separate them from the molds. Place plates over the tops of your molds and flip, then lift the molds off the puddings. Garnish with fruit and mint.

POCKY BISCUIT STICKS

First sold in 1966, Pocky biscuits were invented by Yoshiaki Koma. The chocolate-coated biscuit sticks got their name from *pokkin*, the Japanese mimetic word for the sound of a stick snapping. Since the success of the original Pocky chocolate biscuit, countless different flavors of Pocky are now produced for consumption worldwide, including many varieties sold only during specific times of the year. Attention to seasonality is an important aspect of Japan's pastry culture, and the following Pocky recipes are meant to celebrate the distinct flavors of the different seasons.

AS SEEN IN: *Ga-Rei: Zero; Akame ga Kill!; Hyakko*

In one particularly steamy scene of *Ga-Rei: Zero*, Yomi and Kaura share a passionate kiss after playing the "Pocky Game." An answer to the Western "spaghetti kiss" trope, the Pocky Game is a Japanese party favorite where two people each bite one end of the same Pocky stick. The first one to bite the middle of the Pocky wins, you lose if you let go of the Pocky, and it's a tie if you meet in the middle. Because of the game's popularity and romantic implications, it's a common theme in anime and fan art.

POCKY BISCUIT BASE

Time: 45 minutes • **Yield:** Forty 4-inch stick cookies

4 tablespoons unsalted butter, at room temperature

¼ cup sugar

½ teaspoon vanilla extract

1 large egg

1 cup bread flour plus more for dusting work surface

½ teaspoon baking powder

½ teaspoon salt

4 teaspoons water, at room temperature

1. Preheat your oven to 300°F.

2. In a stand mixer with a paddle attachment, mix together the butter, sugar, and vanilla extract, then add the egg and mix to combine.

3. Sift the flour into a medium bowl and then mix it with the baking powder and salt. Add the dry mixture to the wet mixture in three measures, working the mix into a dough. Add the water and mix the dough until it has a smooth, kneadable consistency.

4. On a clean work surface, sprinkle flour and roll your dough out by hand into thin cylindrical shapes, about 4 to 5 inches long and ¼ inch thick. Use a knife to cut them down to an even length.

5. Place your uncooked Pocky sticks in a row on a large sheet pan lined with parchment paper and bake for 16 minutes, turning the sticks over at 8 minutes. Remove from the oven and let cool.

POCKY COATINGS AND TOPPINGS

When working with chocolate, be sure to use oil-based food coloring and flavor extracts so that the chocolate doesn't crystallize upon contact with moisture and become hard and unworkable!

SPRING/HARU: SAKURA POCKY

1 cup high quality white chocolate, chopped

2 drops oil-based cherry extract

1 tablespoon dried edible sakura blossoms

SUMMER/NATSU: MELON BLACK SUGAR POCKY

1 cup high quality white chocolate, chopped

2 drops oil-based melon extract

2 drops oil-based green food coloring

1 tablespoon crumbled sugar ice cream cone or Okinawan black sugar

AUTUMN/AKI: SWEET POTATO CHESTNUT POCKY

1 cup high quality white chocolate, chopped

½ teaspoon purple sweet potato powder

1 roasted peeled chestnut, finely chopped

WINTER/FUYU: DARK CHOCOLATE ORANGE POCKY

1 cup high quality dark chocolate, chopped

1 tablespoon candied orange peel, chopped

1. To make your preferred chocolate topping: Place the chocolate in a heatproof bowl that fits in your microwave. Heat on medium setting for 30 seconds, then heat in 10-second increments until the chocolate reaches either 110°F on a candy thermometer for milk or white chocolate or 115°F for dark or bittersweet chocolate.

2. Stir your melted chocolate until it cools to between 88° and 90°F for dark chocolate, 84° and 86°F for milk chocolate, or 82° and 84°F for white chocolate. This process of warming and cooling the chocolate is called *tempering*. After tempering, you can test your chocolate by dabbing a bit of it on a piece of parchment paper. Successfully tempered chocolate will harden and display a shine at room temperature. If your chocolate doesn't do these things, continue to mix the chocolate until it reaches a cooler temperature, or heat it in the microwave in 10-second increments until it reaches the correct temperature. Alternatively, you can use untempered melted chocolate for this recipe and store your finished Pocky sticks in the refrigerator.

3. Add your flavor extract (if applicable) and stir to incorporate.

4. Dunk your baked Pocky sticks in the chocolate, using a spoon to ensure all sides of the stick are coated and leaving about ¼ of the stick free of chocolate at one end for easy handling. Rest the coated Pocky on wax paper to cool and sprinkle on your toppings of choice while the chocolate is still wet. Store the finished Pocky in an airtight container.

BANANA MILK

Time: 10 minutes • Yield: 1 glass of banana milk

There is a whole world of bottled drinks to discover inside of Japan's *konbini*, and banana milk is just the tip of the iceberg. Bottled drinks and drink cartons can also be purchased from a wide range of vending machines, many dispensing both cold and warm beverages.

1 banana, peeled

½ cup whole milk

¼ cup water

1 tablespoon honey

½ teaspoon vanilla extract

1. Combine all the ingredients in a blender.

2. Blend on medium speed until all large pieces have been reduced.

3. Enjoy immediately!

AS SEEN IN: *Your Name; After the Rain*

Along with strawberry milk, banana milk has gained a cult following in Japan. In the movie *Your Name*, Mitsuha Miyamizu sips from a box of banana milk as she mulls over her recent erratic behavior with her friends. Mitsuha hasn't been herself recently, and we soon find out that it's because she's been swapping bodies with a teenage boy who lives in Tokyo. Hopefully you're not facing anything quite so perplexing in your life, but if you are, a cup of banana milk will certainly help!

HANAMI DANGO

Time: 30 minutes • **Yield:** 4 *dango* skewers (12 individual dumplings)

Also known as *sanshoku dango* ("san" indicating three colors), *hanami dango* are composed of three colored dumplings served on small bamboo skewers. The white dumpling is meant to represent the last remaining snow of winter, the pink represents cherry blossoms, and the green represents the color of spring and young grass. *Hanami* means "flower viewing" and refers to the Japanese pastime of sitting outside to appreciate the spring sakura flowers, usually accompanied by a picnic. The green dumpling is typically flavored with *yomogi*, or mugwort, a plant that grows wild in Japan. *Yomogi* typically has a darker green appearance than matcha powder. The pink *dango* was originally colored with purple *shiso* (perilla leaf) or pickled sakura blossoms, but now they are more typically colored with pink food coloring, leaving the pink and white dumplings unflavored. In this recipe, we'll use freeze-dried strawberries to achieve a beautiful pink flavored *dango*, as that ingredient is readily available in Western markets. *Hanami dango* also share the celebratory spring colors seen in *Hishi* Mochi (page 85).

One fifth of a16-ounce silken tofu block (about 100 grams)

½ cup *shiratamako*

½ cup *joshinko*

2 tablespoons sugar

½ teaspoon ground mugwort or matcha powder

⅛ cup freeze-dried strawberries, pulsed into a powder in your spice grinder

4 small pastry skewers

1. Fill a small saucepan with water and bring to a boil over medium heat.

2. Mash the silken tofu with a fork in a medium bowl. Then mix together the mashed tofu, *shiratamako*, *joshinko*, and sugar, and knead the ingredients together until a dough forms.

3. Divide the dough into 12 equal balls.

4. Prepare an ice water bath.

5. Knead the mugwort into four of the balls until they are smooth, and knead the strawberry powder into four of the balls until they are smooth.

6. Using a fine mesh sieve, gently deposit the balls into the boiling water.

7. Boil for 3 minutes, stirring occasionally so that the *dango* balls don't stick to the side of your pan. Remove them from the water with a sieve or slotted spoon and immediately place them in the ice water bath to prevent them from overcooking.

8. Wet your small pastry skewers and slide one *dango* ball of each color onto each skewer. Typically, the green *dango* ball goes on first, then white, and finally pink.

AS SEEN IN: *Clannad; Naruto: Shippuden; Touken Ranbu: Hanamaru*

In episode 2 of *Clannad*, Tomoya Okazaki decides to cheer up Nagisa Furukawa by making some *hanami dango* to help draw people to Nagisa's school drama club. This is just the beginning of his efforts to help various girls' wishes come true throughout the series. I suggest making some *hanami dango* the next time you need to impress someone special!

MITARASHI DANGO

Time: 30 minutes • **Yield:** 4 *dango* skewers (12 individual dumplings)

Mitarashi dango are rice dumplings with a sweet soy sauce glaze, typically served on skewers in sets of three. They originated in the Kamo Mitarashi Teahouse in Kyoto, located near the Shimogamo Shrine, and are named after the bubbles in the *mitarashi*, or font of purifying water, found at a shrine's entrance. Over the years, they grew in popularity and are now offered at various teahouses and even in some convenience stores.

DANGO DUMPLINGS

One fifth of a 16-ounce silken tofu block (about 100 grams)

½ cup *shiratamako* or ¼ cup *shiratamako* with ¼ cup *joshinko*

4 small pastry skewers

SAUCE

1 tablespoon soy sauce

2 teaspoons mirin

3 tablespoons water

3 tablespoons sugar or light brown sugar

1 teaspoon potato starch or cornstarch

AS SEEN IN: *Rokuhōdō Yotsuiro Biyori; Charlotte; Samurai Champloo*

In the first few minutes of *Rokuhōdō Yotsuiro Biyori*, viewers are treated to the scrumptious sight of *mitarashi dango* being prepared. At the café Rokuhōdō, owner Sui Tougoku and his strapping coworkers, Gure, Tsubaki, and Tokitaka, are all dedicated to the art of enjoying life through food, especially pastry. As Sui says, "No one needs sweets to survive, but they give you a little bit of relief." A plate of these savory-sweet delights, paired with a cup of tea, is sure to soothe your nerves and add a calming aura to your day.

TO MAKE THE DANGO DUMPLINGS:

1. Fill a small saucepan with water and bring to a boil over medium heat.

2. Mash the silken tofu with a fork in a medium bowl. Then mix together the mashed tofu and *shiratamako*, and knead the ingredients together until a dough forms.

3. Divide the dough into 12 equal balls.

4. Prepare an ice water bath.

5. Using a fine mesh sieve, gently deposit the balls into the boiling water.

6. Boil for 3 minutes, stirring occasionally so that the *dango* dumplings don't stick to the sides of your pan. Remove them from the water with a sieve or slotted spoon and immediately place them in the ice water bath to prevent them from overcooking.

TO MAKE THE SAUCE:

1. Put all of the sauce ingredients in a small pan and stir together until the potato starch dissolves. Place the pan on the stovetop on medium heat and whisk until the sauce begins to thicken. Once the sauce is thick and viscous (about 6 minutes), remove from heat.

2. Wet your small pastry skewers with water and slide the *dango* dumplings onto the skewers, 3 per skewer.

3. Using a grill pan over medium heat, grill each side of the *dango* skewers until marks form. (You can skip this step and move to step number 4 if you want.)

4. Pour the sauce over your *dango* skewers, leaving the blunt end of the skewer free of sauce for gripping.

MUSHROOM CHOCOLATES

Time: 40 minutes prep plus 30 minutes refrigeration • **Yield:** 20 chocolate mushrooms

Composed of a biscuit stem with a chocolate mushroom cap, Kinoko no Yama, or "Mushroom Mountain," is a popular brand of chocolate biscuit sold at convenience stores. The manufacturer also makes Takenoko no Sato, or bamboo-shaped biscuits, which taste identical to Kinoko no Yama (unless you are Sorata Kanda in *The Pet Girl of Sakurasou*). This recipe recreates this snack aisle staple, adding a bit of colorful chocolate flair. You can't help but smile when you're eating chocolate mushrooms!

4 tablespoons unsalted butter, at room temperature

¼ cup sugar

½ teaspoon vanilla extract

1 large egg

½ teaspoon baking powder

1 cup bread flour plus more for dusting work surface

½ teaspoon salt

4 teaspoons water, at room temperature

Twenty 1-inch mini paper baking cups

2½ cups high-quality chopped white chocolate, divided

1 drop oil-based flavor extract (optional)

3 drops red oil-based food coloring

1. Preheat your oven to 300°F.

2. In a large mixing bowl, mix together the butter, sugar, and vanilla extract. Add the egg and baking powder and stir to combine. Then add the flour and salt in stages, working the mix into a dough with a wooden spoon. Finally, add the water and mix the dough until it has a smooth, kneadable consistency.

3. On a clean work surface, sprinkle flour and roll out your dough into at least twenty 1½-inch-long-by-¼-inch-wide cylindrical shapes. Use a knife to cut the mushroom stems down to a consistent size, then place them on a large sheet pan lined with parchment paper.

4. Bake for 14 minutes, turning the pan around halfway through. Remove from the oven and let cool.

5. Arrange twenty 1-inch mini paper baking cups on a large sheet pan.

6. Separate ¼ cup of white chocolate and place it in a small heatproof bowl, and place the remaining 2¼ cups of white chocolate in a medium heatproof bowl.

The Pet Girl of Sakurasou focuses on Mashiro Shiina, a world-famous artist with no common sense, and Sorata Kanda, a boy who takes it upon himself to help her. In episode 15, Sorata is offered some chocolate biscuits shaped like mushrooms but says that he prefers the ones shaped like bamboo shoots. Later, in episode 17, Mashiro gives Sorata a box of bamboo shoot chocolates on Valentine's Day, remembering that he prefers that shape.

7. Heat the ¼ cup of chocolate in the microwave on medium setting for 30 seconds. Microwave for another 30 seconds, then 15 seconds, then 10 seconds, until the chocolate can be stirred to a smooth consistency. Add oil-based flavor extract, if desired, and stir to incorporate.

8. Fill a piping bag with the melted chocolate and cut a very small hole at the tip. Pipe polka dots onto the bottom and sides of each paper baking cup. Refrigerate the baking cups for 10 minutes.

9. Microwave the remaining 2¼ cups of chocolate until it is smooth, using the method described in step 7 above. Add red oil-based food coloring, mix to incorporate, and pipe the now-red chocolate into each baking cup, about ¾ full.

10. Place one stem biscuit into each mold while the red chocolate is still wet, and chill for 30 minutes before removing the mushrooms from their wrappers. For optimal flavor, let them sit for 10 minutes at room temperature before eating.

YŌKAN

Time: 15 minutes plus 3 hours chilling time • **Yield:** 12 *yōkan* squares

Yōkan, or *mizu yōkan*, is red bean jelly, though there are a variety of other flavors as well, including sweet potato *yōkan* and red bean *yōkan* with chestnuts. *Yōkan* is one of the simplest combinations of ingredients: water, kanten powder, smooth red bean paste, and a little bit of salt and sugar. In this version, I add floral-shaped cutouts from baked *satsumaimo* (sweet potato) for additional texture and flavor.

Nonstick cooking spray

1 cup water

1 teaspoon kanten powder or agar

2 tablespoons sugar

1 pinch salt

1½ cups *koshi an* (smooth Red Bean Paste, page 12)

½ cup cooked *satsumaimo*, cut into fun floral shapes

1. Spray an 8-by-8-inch cake or brownie pan with a thin layer of nonstick cooking spray, then prepare an ice water bath in a heatproof bowl large enough to fit the saucepan you will be using in step 2.

2. In a medium saucepan over medium heat, combine the water and the kanten powder and bring it to a boil while whisking. Once the mixture is boiling, turn the heat down to low. Remove from heat after 2 minutes.

3. Add the sugar, salt, and *koshi an*, and continue mixing until they are completely incorporated and the mixture is smooth. Return the pan to medium heat and bring to a boil once more. Then remove from the heat and place the pan immediately in the ice water bath to halt the cooking process.

4. Pour the red bean mixture into your prepared cake pan and place your cooked *satsumaimo* pieces on top of the bean mixture.

5. Refrigerate for at least 3 hours before cutting into pieces.

AS SEEN IN: *Elegant Yokai Apartment Life; Tsugumomo; Is the Order a Rabbit?*

In episode 9 of *Elegant Yokai Apartment Life*, a *tengu* (a type of legendary Japanese folk creature with wings) named Matajuro visits the apartment and talks about his life in the mountains. Ruriko brings out a piece of perfectly cut *yōkan* to serve with a cup of tea as Matajuro-san entertains the group. Your guests will be in for a treat as well if you make *yōkan* for your next gathering!

ICHIGO DAIFUKU

Time: 25 minutes • **Yield:** 6 *ichigo daifuku*

Ichigo daifuku is a popular spring *wagashi* made with mochi, the sticky dough that forms from cooking glutinous rice with sugar and water. In this version, I make the outer layer of mochi pink to evoke spring petals, but *ichigo daifuku* typically has a white mochi covering, so feel free to skip the food coloring if you want to achieve this more quintessential appearance. You can also make your *ichigo daifuku* with other fillings, like matcha custard, another excellent pairing with ripe strawberries. Once you've made *ichigo daifuku*, try your hand at different varieties of fruit *daifuku*, such as tangerine or kiwi!

MOCHI

½ cup *mochiko*

¼ cup *shiratamako*

¼ cup sugar

⅔ cup water

Pink food coloring (optional)

½ cup cornstarch or potato starch
for dusting

FILLING

6 ripe whole strawberries, hulled
(smaller berries work best)

1 cup *anko* (Red Bean Paste, page 12),
divided into 6 pieces and chilled

TO MAKE THE MOCHI:

1. Wash the strawberries and dry them completely.

2. Place the *mochiko*, *shiratamako*, and sugar in a large bowl, add the water and food coloring, and mix. Cover the bowl with plastic wrap and microwave on medium setting for 2 minutes. Remove from the microwave and mix to combine, then microwave for 1 additional minute.

3. Spread cornstarch or potato starch on a flat work surface. Dump the mochi dough onto the surface and divide it into 6 equal pieces. Using a small plastic rolling pin, roll each piece until it is round and flat. You may want to sprinkle a light layer of cornstarch on top of the dough before rolling.

TO MAKE THE FILLING:

1. Surround each strawberry with roughly ⅙ of your *anko*.

2. Place an *anko*-covered strawberry on each mochi piece with the tip facing down and wrap the mochi around it. Pinch the edges of the mochi closed and place the *daifuku* seam side down on a clean plate or tray.

3. Refrigerate for 10 minutes and enjoy right away.

AS SEEN IN: *March Comes in Like a Lion; Laid-Back Camp*

In episode 21 of *March Comes in Like a Lion*, the Kawamoto sisters brainstorm with their grandfather to come up with a new summer treat to sell at his *wagashi* shop. Hinata suggests something similar to *ichigo daifuku,* which doesn't have a long shelf life but is very popular. They end up deciding on a *daruma* (doll) shaped *daifuku*, which is filled with multiple flavors of bean jam. Once you master the strawberry version of *daifuku*, you'll want to experiment with form and flavor just like the Kawamoto family!

SAKURA MOCHI

Time: 30 minutes plus overnight soaking • **Yield:** 6 pieces

Sakura mochi are a spring *wagashi*, and they get most of their sakura flavor from a pickled young sakura leaf that is wrapped around the mochi ball. You eat the leaf! These mochi are eaten in celebration of Hinamatsuri, or Girls' Day, as well as more broadly during cherry blossom season in Japan. They are meant to invite good luck and health to the girls in the family. In this version, I top the mochi with pickled sakura blossoms rather than leaves because they are more readily available from online sources. You can also add a few drops of sakura extract to the mochi and decorate them with candied edible blossoms from your local farmers market, though this is less traditional in form.

There are two varieties of sakura mochi: *domyoji* sakura mochi and *chomeiji* sakura mochi. *Domyoji* sakura mochi is traced back to the Kansai region of Japan. For its exterior, it uses sweet glutinous rice broken into smaller pieces, or *domyojiko*. The recipe below is for *domyoji* sakura mochi. You can choose to mash the rice during the cooking process, or substitute *domyojiko* for the glutinous rice, which can be sourced at Japanese grocery stores. *Chomeiji* sakura mochi has roots in the Kanto region. Instead of a sticky rice exterior, it is wrapped in a pink pancake made with wheat flour, *shiratamako*, sugar, and water.

FILLING

Pickled sakura blossoms
   (sometimes sold as sakura tea)

6 pickled sakura leaves (optional)

6 tablespoons *anko* (Red Bean Paste,
   page 12), chilled

Edible flowers, candied and dunked
   in egg white and sugar (optional)

DOMYOJI MOCHI

1 cup glutinous rice, soaked overnight

½ cup water

2 tablespoons sugar

2 drops pink gel food coloring

AS SEEN IN: *Tamako Market; Elegant Yokai Apartment Life; Demon Slayer*

In episode 3 of *Tamako Market*, Tamako Kitashirakawa is making sakura mochi at her family's shop at the Usagiyama Market when she is visited by Shiori, a shy girl in her class. Shiori stays for dinner with the family, and the two girls become friends. Celebrate new beginnings with a sakura mochi, just like Tamako!

TO MAKE THE FILLING:

1. Soak the pickled sakura blossoms or leaves in cool water for 15 minutes to remove excess salt.

2. Roll the *anko* into 6 balls of equal size and refrigerate.

TO MAKE THE DOMYOJI MOCHI:

1. Place the rice, ½ cup of water, the sugar, and the pink gel food coloring in a medium microwave-safe bowl and cover with a layer of plastic wrap. Microwave for 6 minutes on medium setting, pausing halfway through to mix with a rubber spatula so that the mixture doesn't harden on the sides of the bowl.

2. Remove from the microwave and mix vigorously, so that the rice begins to mash together and the color is evenly distributed. Do not mash the rice completely; you want to retain some rice chunk definition with this kind of mochi.

3. Divide the *domyoji* mochi into 6 equal balls. Covering the palm of your nondominant hand with a piece of plastic wrap, flatten a ball of mochi against it using your other hand. Place a ball of the *anko* inside the flattened mochi, and use the plastic wrap to mold the rice around it.

4. If you have pickled sakura leaves, wrap one around each mochi ball, with the smooth side facing the mochi. If you are using sakura blossoms, delicately garnish each ball, patting the flower down so that it sticks to the rice.

5. Chill for 10 minutes before serving.

FROM THE
PANYA

MELON PAN

Melon *pan* features a signature sugar-covered cookie coating that is baked around fluffy sweet milk bread. (The word *pan*, or "bread" in Japanese, is derived from the Portuguese word for bread, *pão*.) Sold predominantly at bakeries and convenience stores in Japan, these round buns get their name from their classic melon shape rather than from their flavor—although some shops do sell melon-flavored melon *pan*. This versatile treat can be creatively sculpted and flavored to fit almost any mood. In the following recipes, you will make strawberry-flavored buns that are also shaped like a strawberry, classically shaped melon *pan* with a matcha topping, and melon *pan* in the shape of a *kawaii* bunny face!

AS SEEN IN: *Shokugan no Shana; One Week Friends; Gabriel Dropout*

In the world of *Shokugan no Shana*, Shana is a fierce warrior known as a "Flame Haze" who battles enigmatic beings called Crimson Denizens from a parallel universe. Although her single-minded focus on eradicating these monsters makes her seem cold and uncaring, Shana does have a softer side as well. In particular, she has a weak spot for melon *pan*—and after you try out this recipe, you will too!

ICHIGO MELON PAN

Time: 3 hours • **Yield:** 8 buns

BREAD DOUGH

1¾ cups bread flour

¼ cup cake flour

1 large pinch salt

3 tablespoons sugar

1¼ teaspoons instant dry yeast

1 large egg

3½ tablespoons water, at room temperature

4½ tablespoons whole milk, at room temperature

2½ tablespoons unsalted butter, cut into ½-inch cubes, at room temperature

Nonstick cooking spray

COOKIE TOPPING

4 tablespoons unsalted butter, cubed

1 cup sugar, divided

1 large egg

2 teaspoons strawberry extract

1 cup all-purpose flour

1 pinch salt

½ teaspoon baking powder

Pink and green gel food coloring

1 cup strawberry yogurt baking chips

TO MAKE THE BREAD DOUGH:

1. In a stand mixer with a dough hook attachment, add all of the dry ingredients and mix to combine on low speed.

2. Beat the egg in a separate bowl, then add the egg, water, and milk to the dry ingredients. Continue to mix on medium speed as the mixture begins to combine, about 2 minutes.

3. Add the cubed butter and continue to mix on medium speed for about 10 minutes. The dough should become elastic and stretch when pulled in two directions. If the dough is too dry, add an extra tablespoon of milk.

4. Spray the inside of a medium heatproof bowl with nonstick cooking spray. Place the dough inside and cover with plastic wrap. If your oven has a proof setting, let the dough rest and proof in the oven at roughly 100°F for 1 hour 30 minutes. If not, let the dough rest for 2 hours at room temperature.

TO MAKE THE COOKIE TOPPING:

1. While the dough is resting, combine the butter and ½ cup sugar together in a stand mixer with a paddle attachment, beating until light and fluffy, about 2 minutes. Then add the egg and the strawberry extract and mix to combine.

2. In a separate medium bowl, sift the flour and whisk it together with the salt and baking powder. Add this dry mixture to the wet mixture in two stages, mixing to form a dough.

3. Divide the cookie dough into 4 equal pieces. Color half of the dough (2 pieces) with pink food coloring, kneading the color into the dough on a clean work surface. Color a quarter of the dough (1 piece) with green food coloring in the same way. Keep the other quarter of the dough its natural beige color.

4. Wrap the cookie dough in plastic wrap and refrigerate until needed.

5. Once the bread dough has proofed for 1 hour 30 minutes, pour it onto a work surface sprinkled with flour. Divide the dough into 8 equal sized triangle shapes (around 75 grams each) and place an equal portion of the yogurt chips on each piece of dough. Gather the edges of the dough together into a ball shape, enclosing the yogurt chips and forming a seam at the bottom of the 6 buns. Pinch the seams closed and place the buns seam side down on a large parchment-lined sheet pan.

6. Cover the buns with plastic wrap and proof in the oven at 100°F for an additional 50 minutes, if your oven has a proof setting. If not, proof at room temperature until the dough has almost doubled in size, about 1 hour.

7. Preheat the oven to 350°F.

8. Roll out your pieces of cookie dough topping to about $\frac{1}{8}$ inch thick. Cut the pink dough into 8 separate pieces (triangle shapes work best). Wrap this dough around your proofed buns, tucking the edges underneath the side of each bun.

9. Cut out strawberry leaf and stem designs from the green dough. Place this dough on top of the pink buns and pat it down to affix.

10 Form small round dough pieces (between $\frac{1}{8}$ and $\frac{1}{4}$ inch) with the uncolored dough and distribute on each bun to mimic strawberry seeds. Pat down to affix.

11. Pour the remaining $\frac{1}{2}$ cup sugar into a small dish. Gently roll each bun in the sugar so that its top cookie surface is covered.

12. Place the buns on a baking tray lined with parchment paper, evenly spaced about 2 inches apart. Bake for 17 minutes.

BUNNY FACE MELON PAN

Time: 3 hours • **Yield:** 6 buns

BREAD DOUGH

1¾ cups bread flour

¼ cup cake flour

1 large pinch salt

3 tablespoons sugar

1¼ teaspoons instant dry yeast

1 large egg

3½ tablespoons water, at room temperature

4½ tablespoons whole milk, at room temperature

2½ tablespoons unsalted butter, cut into ½-inch cubes, at room temperature

Nonstick cooking spray

COOKIE TOPPING

4 tablespoons unsalted butter, cubed

1 cup sugar, divided

1 large egg

1 cup all-purpose flour

1 pinch salt

½ teaspoon baking powder

Black gel food coloring

1 tablespoon pink sanding sugar (colored decorative sugar)

TO MAKE THE BREAD DOUGH:

1. In a stand mixer with a dough hook attachment, add all of the dry ingredients and mix to combine on low speed.

2. Beat the egg in a separate bowl, then add the egg, water, and milk to the dry ingredients. Continue to mix on medium speed as the mixture begins to combine, about 2 minutes.

3. Add the cubed butter and continue to mix on medium speed for about 10 minutes. The dough should become elastic and stretch when pulled in two directions. If the dough is too dry, add an extra tablepoon of milk.

4. Spray the inside of a medium heatproof bowl with nonstick cooking spray. Place the dough inside and cover with plastic wrap. If your oven has a proof setting, let the dough rest and proof in the oven at roughly 100°F for 1 hour 30 minutes. If not, let the dough rest for 2 hours at room temperature.

TO MAKE THE COOKIE TOPPING:

1. While the dough is proofing, cream the butter and $\frac{1}{2}$ cup sugar together in a stand mixer with a paddle attachment, about 2 minutes. Then add the egg and mix to combine.

2. In a separate medium bowl, sift the flour and whisk it together with the salt and baking powder. Add this dry mixture to the wet mixture in two stages, mixing to form a dough.

3. Reserve $\frac{1}{4}$ cup of the cookie dough and knead 1 drop of black food coloring into that portion. Reserve an additional $\frac{1}{2}$ cup of cookie dough; this will become the bunny ears. Wrap the pieces of cookie dough in plastic wrap and refrigerate until needed.

4. Once the bread dough has proofed for 1 hour 30 minutes, pour it onto a work surface sprinkled with flour. Divide the dough into 6 equal sized triangle shapes (around 100 grams each) and gather the edges of the dough together to create a ball shape. Pinch the seams closed and place the buns seam side down on a large parchment-lined sheet pan.

5. Cover the buns with plastic wrap and let them proof in the oven at 100°F for an additional 50 minutes, if your oven has a proof setting. If not, proof at room temperature until the dough has almost doubled in size, about 1 hour.

6. Preheat the oven to 350°F.

7. Roll out your pieces of cookie dough topping to about $\frac{1}{8}$ inch thick. Mold the black dough into 12 small black dots for the eyes and 12 thin dough lines to create small x shapes for the noses. Cut out 12 ear shapes from the reserved uncolored dough and shape with your hands.

8. Cut the other piece of uncolored cookie dough into 6 separate squares. Surround each bun with a square of cookie dough, tucking the dough under each bun.

9. Pour the remaining $\frac{1}{2}$ cup sugar into a small dish and roll the cookie dough top of each bun in the sugar.

10. Place the bunny ears underneath each bun. Sprinkle each ear with pink sanding sugar (a variety of colored decorative sugar).

11. Using a small food-safe paintbrush, moisten the areas of the dough where you would like to position each eye and nose, then place the black dough eye and nose pieces and pat down to affix. Use additional pink sanding sugar to create a blush effect on each bunny cheek, if desired.

12. Place the buns on a baking tray lined with parchment paper, evenly spaced about 2 inches apart. Bake for 17 minutes.

MATCHA MELON PAN

Time: 3 hours • **Yield:** 6 buns

BREAD DOUGH

1¾ cups bread flour

¼ cup cake flour

1 large pinch salt

3 tablespoons sugar

1¼ teaspoons instant dry yeast

1 large egg

3½ tablespoons water, at room temperature

4½ tablespoons whole milk, at room temperature

2½ tablespoons unsalted butter, cut into ½-inch cubes, at room temperature

Nonstick cooking spray

COOKIE TOPPING

4 tablespoons unsalted butter, cubed

1 cup sugar, divided

1 large egg

1 cup all-purpose flour

1 pinch salt

2 teaspoons matcha powder

½ teaspoon baking powder

TO MAKE THE BREAD DOUGH:

1. In a stand mixer with a dough hook attachment, add all of the dry ingredients and mix to combine on low speed.

2. Beat the egg in a separate bowl, then add the egg, water, and milk to the dry ingredients. Continue to mix on medium speed as the mixture begins to combine, about 2 minutes.

3. Add the cubed butter and continue to mix on medium speed for about 10 minutes. The dough should become elastic and stretch when pulled in two directions. If the dough is too dry, add an extra tablespoon of milk.

4. Spray the inside of a medium heatproof bowl with nonstick cooking spray. Place the dough inside and cover with plastic wrap. If your oven has a proof setting, let the dough rest and proof in the oven at roughly 100°F for 1 hour 30 minutes. If not, let the dough rest for 2 hours at room temperature.

TO MAKE THE COOKIE TOPPING:

1. While the dough is proofing, cream the butter and ½ cup sugar together in a stand mixer with a paddle attachment, about 2 minutes. Then add the egg and mix to combine.

2. In a separate medium bowl, sift the flour and whisk it together with the salt, matcha powder, and baking powder. Add this dry mixture to the wet mixture in two stages, mixing to form a dough.

3. Wrap the cookie dough in plastic wrap and refrigerate until needed.

4. Once the bread dough has proofed for 1 hour 30 minutes, pour it onto a work surface sprinkled with flour. Divide the dough into 6 equal sized triangle shapes (around 100 grams each) and gather the edges of the dough together to create a ball shape. Pinch the seams closed and place the buns seam side down on a large parchment-lined sheet pan.

5. Cover the buns with plastic wrap and let them proof in the oven at 100°F for an additional 50 minutes, if your oven has a proof setting. If not, proof at room temperature until the dough has almost doubled in size, about 1 hour.

6. Preheat the oven to 350°F.

7. Roll out your cookie dough topping to about ⅛ inch thick. Cut the dough into 6 separate square pieces. Gently wrap these pieces around your proofed buns.

8. Score each bun with a crosshatch pattern, using a knife or bench scraper, taking care to not cut too deeply into the main melon *pan* dough.

9. Pour the remaining ½ cup sugar into a small dish and roll the cookie dough top of each bun in the sugar.

10. Place the buns on a baking tray lined with parchment paper, evenly spaced about 2 inches apart. Bake for 17 minutes.

MELON PAN ICE CREAM SANDO

Time: 5 minutes • **Yield:** 1 ice cream sandwich

AS SEEN IN: *Gatchaman Crowds Insight*

In episode 2 of *Gatchaman Crowds Insight*, Hajime Ichinose orders a decadent dish consisting of soft-serve vanilla ice cream sandwiched between two sides of a melon *pan* bun. What a treat to order before 7 a.m.! Hajime is known for her positive outlook—perhaps some of it is thanks to her high sugar intake.

In recent years, melon *pan* ice cream sandwiches have soared in popularity in Japan. You can decide for yourself when is the best time to indulge in this treat (7 a.m. ice cream isn't for everyone), but whenever you eat it, it will undoubtedly give you an uplifting dose of positive energy!

1 Melon *Pan* bun (page 48)

2 large strawberries, hulled and thinly sliced

1 pint adzuki (red bean) ice cream or your flavor of choice

1 tablespoon rainbow sprinkles

1. Using a bread knife, carefully cut your Melon *Pan* bun in half horizontally so that the cookie crumble top is intact, and arrange the sliced strawberries on the bottom half of the bun.

2. Using a bread knife, cut a ½-inch slice horizontally off the top of an entire cold adzuki ice cream pint (with the lid removed but with the the wrapper still on). Wrap the remaining partial pint of ice cream in plastic wrap and place it back into the freezer, then peel the wrapper and carton off of the ½-inch slice and place it on the bottom half of the bun.

3. Place the top cookie half of the bun on your ice cream sando. Wrap half of your ice cream sandwich with a piece of parchment paper for easy gripping.

4. Sprinkle the top of the sandwich with rainbow sprinkles. Eat immediately.

SHOKUPAN

Time: 3 hours • **Yield:** One 8½-by-4½-by-4½-inch loaf

Shokupan is a soft white bread made using milk or milk powder and is the most popular bread in Japan. It has a yielding but bouncy texture and is usually more thickly sliced (*atsugiri*) than Western loaves. *Shokupan* is used to make *Ogura* Toast (page 55), a specialty of the Nagoya area consisting of thick-cut toasted *shokupan*, *ogura* jam (similar to *tsubu an* bean paste), and butter. Another well-known *shokupan* creation is Shibuya Honey Toast (page 56), which is especially popular as a shared dish among the young and hip. (Shibuya is a fashionable Tokyo neighborhood that is famed for its shopping and nightlife.) *Shokupan* Fruit Sandos (page 57) are sweet *shokupan* sandwiches filled with seasonal fruit and whipped cream that often reveal designs when sliced diagonally. They are a light and sweet dessert and are typically sold alongside savory sandwiches.

STARTER

¹/₃ cup whole milk

3 tablespoons bread flour

SHOKUPAN

1 tablespoon active dry yeast

²/₃ cup whole milk, heated to 110°F

2 cups bread flour

½ cup cake flour

¼ cup sugar

1 large pinch salt

1 large egg

4 tablespoons unsalted butter, at room temperature

Nonstick cooking spray

EGG WASH

1 large egg

1 tablespoon whole milk

AS SEEN IN: *Shokupan Mimi; Aldnoah.Zero; Restaurant to Another World*

The title character of the children's anime *Shokupan Mimi* is a girl made out of *shokupan* bread who likes to be fashionable, which in her case means suntanning in a toaster, using jam as makeup, and pining after Breadsome-kun, a handsome croissant. Recreate the likeness of *Shokupan* Mimi with this fluffy bread recipe, and soon your world, too, will revolve around bread!

TO MAKE THE STARTER:

1. In a medium saucepan over high heat, combine the whole milk and the bread flour. Whisk until a paste begins to form, about 1 minute. Remove from heat.

TO MAKE THE SHOKUPAN:

1. Activate the yeast by pouring it into the ²/₃ cup warm milk, letting it rest for 5 minutes.

2. In a stand mixer, mix the bread flour, cake flour, sugar, and salt until combined. Then add the egg, the yeast mixture, and the starter mixture and mix on medium speed using a dough hook. As an elastic dough forms, add the butter 1 tablespoon at a time. The dough should become smooth and stretchy as it is worked, about 5 minutes. If the dough is too dry, add an additional tablespoon of milk.

3. Place the dough in a large bowl sprayed with nonstick cooking spray and cover with plastic wrap. Let it rest and double in size, about 1 hour.

4. Form the dough into two circular buns of equal size. Cover with a wet paper towel and let them rest at room temperature for an additional 30 minutes.

5. Preheat your oven to 350°F.

6. Spray the inside of an 8½-by-4½-by-4½-inch loaf pan with nonstick cooking spray, and place the two buns side by side in the pan.

TO MAKE THE EGG WASH:

1. In a small bowl, mix the egg and milk together. Gently brush the egg wash onto the top of your loaf with a pastry brush.

2. Bake for 35 minutes, or until the top crust is a deep golden brown color.

3. Let cool before removing the loaf from the pan, and then let it rest for at least 1 hour before cutting slices with a bread knife. If you slice too soon, you may disrupt the interior texture of the bread.

OGURA TOAST

Time: 10 minutes • **Yield:** 1 slice of toast

One 1-inch slice of *Shokupan* (page 54)

3 tablespoons *tsubu an* (coarse Red Bean Paste, page 12)
or *ogura* jam (prepared in the same manner as *tsubu an* but
keeping the beans intact)

1 tablespoon salted butter, cold, cut with a cookie cutter
into a heart shape

1 teaspoon *kinako* (optional)

1. Toast the *Shokupan* slice under your broiler for about
   1 minute, monitoring so that it doesn't burn.

2. Using an offset spatula or spoon, apply a thick layer of
   tsubu an or *ogura* jam to the middle of the toast.

3. Place your heart-shaped butter pat on top and sift on *kinako*
   using a fine mesh sieve, if desired.

4. Enjoy with your morning tea or coffee.

SHIBUYA HONEY TOAST

Time: 30 minutes • **Yield:** 1 toast tower, best shared between 2 people

One 8½-by-4½-by-4½-inch loaf (page 54)

3 tablespoons unsalted butter, melted and divided

¼ cup sugar

3 tablespoons sweetened condensed milk

2 scoops matcha ice cream

¼ cup strawberries, hulled and quartered

¼ cup blueberries

3 Pocky Biscuit Sticks (page 34), any flavor

Your favorite Japanese snacks for garnishing (such as Koala's March cookies)

Whipped cream for garnishing

1. Preheat your oven to 350°F and line a large sheet pan with parchment paper.

2. Remove a 1-inch end slice from the loaf of *Shokupan*. Then, leaving the other 5 sides intact, carve a rectangle out of the *Shokupan* from the crustless side of the loaf, leaving a ½-inch border on all sides to create a bread bowl shape.

3. Remove the interior bread and cut it into 1-inch cubes with a bread knife.

4. Using a pastry brush, apply 2 tablespoons of melted butter to the inside walls of the hollowed-out loaf. Toss the bread cubes from the inside of the loaf in the remaining 1 tablespoon of melted butter and sprinkle sugar onto the cubes.

5. Place both the loaf and the bread cubes on the sheet pan and bake for 15 minutes.

6. Remove the toasted bread cubes from the sheet pan, then center the loaf on the pan and bake for an additional 10 minutes, or until it is golden around the edges.

7. Brush the inside of the toasted loaf with sweetened condensed milk, then reinsert the toasted cubes into the loaf.

8. Top with matcha ice cream and berries, and garnish with snacks such as Pocky, Koala's March cookies, or *Dango* Dumplings (pages 37–38), as well as whipped cream to taste.

SHOKUPAN FRUIT SANDO

Time: 30 minutes • **Yield:** 1 fruit sando

1 cup heavy whipping cream

2 tablespoons powdered sugar

Two 1½-inch-thick slices of *Shokupan* (page 54)

1 cup chopped fresh fruits (such as kiwi, mandarin orange, or strawberry)

1. In a chilled bowl, whip heavy whipping cream on medium speed with a stand mixer. Once frothy (about 1 minute), add powdered sugar. Then continue to whip until soft peaks form.

2. With an offset spatula or spoon, spread an evenly thick layer of whipped cream on one slice of your *Shokupan* bread and place a layer of chopped fresh fruit onto the whipped cream.

3. Spread a thick layer of whipped cream on the other slice of bread and put the two pieces of bread together. Gently wrap with plastic wrap and chill for 20 minutes.

4. Using a bread knife, remove the crusts from the bread. Then slice the sando diagonally, forming two triangular pieces.

CORNETS

Cornets are typically filled with chocolate or custard cream and are the most popular type of *chokopan* (chocolate bread) in Japan. You will need a cone-shaped baking mold to make this recipe.

AS SEEN IN: *Lucky Star; Rascal Does Not Dream of Bunny Girl Senpai; Cardfight!! Vanguard G; BanG Dream!*

As she bites into a chocolate cornet in episode 1 of *Lucky Star*, Konata Izumi muses with her friend Tsukasa Hiiragi about the best way to consume the shell-shaped dessert. Should you start at the head or at the tail? Which end would be considered the head? Is there really a proper way to eat these delectable treats? The only way to answer these questions is to make them for yourself!

CHOCOLATE CORNET

Time: 2 hours 20 minutes • **Yield:** 6 cornet cream horns

CORNET HORN

1 teaspoon active dry yeast

1 tablespoon water, lukewarm

1¼ cups bread flour

1 tablespoon sugar

½ tablespoon whole milk

1 tablespoon egg, beaten

⅓ cup water

1½ tablespoons unsalted butter, cubed

Nonstick cooking spray

CHOCOLATE CREAM

2 large egg yolks

2½ tablespoons sugar

1 tablespoon cake flour

1 tablespoon cocoa powder

1 tablespoon cornstarch

1 cup whole milk

¼ cup semisweet chocolate chips

1 tablespoon unsalted butter

EGG WASH

1 large egg yolk, beaten

1 tablespoon whole milk

½ cup powdered sugar for garnishing

TO MAKE THE CORNET HORN:

1. Prepare a large sheet pan with parchment paper.

2. In a small bowl, dissolve the yeast in the lukewarm water for about 5 minutes. In a medium bowl, whisk together the bread flour, sugar, and milk, then mix the yeast mixture into the flour mixture using a spatula.

3. In another small bowl, combine the egg and water and mix them into the flour mixture.

4. Transfer the mixture to a stand mixer with a dough hook attachment and mix on medium speed for 5 minutes. You can also use a food processor and pulse for 30-second intervals, until a dough ball begins to form. Add the cubed butter and mix until the dough is smooth and elastic, about 10 minutes.

5. Place the dough in a large bowl greased with nonstick cooking spray and sprinkle flour over the top. Cover with plastic wrap and let the dough rest and rise for 1 hour.

TO MAKE THE CHOCOLATE CREAM:

1. While waiting for the dough to rise, combine the egg yolks with the sugar in a medium bowl and whisk together. In a separate bowl, combine the cake flour, cocoa powder, and cornstarch, and add these dry ingredients to the egg mixture. Mix to combine.

2. In a medium saucepan, bring milk to a simmer over medium-low heat. Slowly incorporate the hot milk into the egg mixture, then strain the mixture and pour it into a medium saucepan. Whisk over medium heat until the mixture begins to thicken, about 3 minutes.

3. Remove from heat and add the chocolate chips and unsalted butter. Mix together until they are incorporated, then pour the chocolate cream through a fine mesh sieve into a medium bowl and let it cool at room temperature for 10 minutes.

4. Cover your mixture with plastic wrap, making sure the plastic wrap is in contact with the cream so that a skin doesn't form on its surface, and refrigerate.

5. Once your dough has doubled in size, poke it with your finger to check if it's ready. If the hole disappears quickly, your dough needs more rising time.

6. Remove the dough from its bowl and place it on a floured surface. Pat the dough to remove some of the larger air bubbles, then divide it into 6 equal pieces. Shape and tuck the pieces into 6 balls and let them rest under a wet paper towel for 15 to 20 minutes.

7. Roll each dough ball out into a long strip of a uniform width, about 9 inches long and 1½ inches wide. Wrap the dough strips around upright greased cone molds in a spiral pattern, creating a shell shape. Don't feel like you need to extend the dough strips all the way to the rim of the cone; try to wind them around the mold three times.

8. Place the horns on the parchment paper and cover the entire tray with plastic. Let them rise for 30 minutes, until the dough has puffed up and doubled in size.

9. Preheat your oven to 350°F.

TO MAKE THE EGG WASH:

1. Mix the egg yolk with the milk, then brush each horn with the egg wash. Bake for 16 minutes, or until the dough is golden. Once the horns have cooled, remove them from the molds and fill a piping bag with the chocolate cream. Using a round tip, pipe the chocolate cream into each cornet horn.

2. Dust with powdered sugar using a fine mesh sieve.

BANANA MILK CORNET

Time: 4 hours 20 minutes (includes banana custard infusion time) • **Yield:** 6 cornet cream horns

CORNET HORN

1 teaspoon active dry yeast

1 tablespoon water, lukewarm

1¼ cups bread flour

1 tablespoon sugar

½ tablespoon dry milk powder

1 tablespoon egg, beaten

⅓ cup water

1½ tablespoons unsalted butter, cubed

Nonstick cooking spray

BANANA CUSTARD

2 medium bananas, peeled and mashed

1¾ cups whole milk

1 teaspoon vanilla extract

½ cup sugar

3 tablespoons cornstarch

¼ teaspoon salt

5 large egg yolks

EGG WASH

1 egg yolk, beaten

1 tablespoon whole milk

½ cup cocoa powder for garnishing

TO MAKE THE CORNET HORNS

1. Prepare a large sheet pan with parchment paper.

2. In a small bowl, dissolve the yeast in the lukewarm water for about 5 minutes. In a medium bowl, whisk together the bread flour, sugar, and milk powder, then mix the yeast mixture into the flour mixture using a spatula.

3. In another small bowl, combine the egg and water and mix them into the flour mixture.

4. Transfer the mixture to a stand mixer with a dough hook attachment and mix on medium speed for 5 minutes. You can also use a food processor and pulse for 30-second intervals, until a dough ball begins to form. Add the cubed butter and mix until the dough is smooth and elastic, about 10 minutes.

5. Place the dough in a large bowl greased with nonstick cooking spray and sprinkle flour over the top. Cover with plastic wrap and let the dough rest and rise for 1 hour.

TO MAKE THE BANANA CUSTARD:

1. While waiting for your dough to rise, combine the mashed bananas with the milk in a medium saucepan and bring to a simmer over medium heat. Remove from heat and transfer to a medium bowl. Cover with plastic wrap and refrigerate for at least 4 hours.

2. After chilling, bring the banana mixture back to a simmer in a medium saucepan over medium heat, then strain it into a medium bowl using a fine mesh sieve.

3. In the same saucepan you used earlier, whisk together the vanilla extract, sugar, cornstarch, salt, and egg yolks. Whisk in your infused banana milk and return to the stove over low heat.

4. Whisk for about 5 minutes and then bring the mixture to medium heat. Continue whisking for 5 minutes as the custard thickens. When it reaches your desired thickness, take it off the heat and transfer it to a bowl. Cover it with plastic wrap, making sure the plastic wrap is in contact with the custard so that a skin doesn't form on its surface, and refrigerate.

5. Once your dough has doubled in size, poke it with your finger to check if it's ready. If the hole disappears quickly, your dough needs more rising time.

6. Remove the dough from its bowl and place it on a floured surface. Pat the dough to remove some of the larger air bubbles, then divide it into 6 equal pieces. Shape and tuck the pieces into 6 balls and let them rest under a wet paper towel for 15 to 20 minutes.

7. Roll each dough ball out into a long strip of a uniform width, about 9 inches long and 1½ inches wide. Wrap the dough strips around upright greased cone molds in a spiral pattern, creating a shell shape. Don't feel like you need to extend the dough strips all the way to the rim of the cone; try to wind them around the mold three times.

8. Place the horns on the parchment paper and cover the entire tray with plastic. Let them rise for 30 minutes, until the dough has puffed up and doubled in size.

9. Preheat your oven to 350°F.

TO MAKE THE EGG WASH:

1. Mix the egg yolk with the milk, then brush each horn with the egg wash. Bake for 16 minutes, or until the dough is golden. Once the horns have cooled, remove them from the molds and fill a piping bag with the banana custard. Using a round tip, pipe the banana custard into each cornet horn.

2. Dust with cocoa powder using a fine mesh sieve, and enjoy with a glass of Banana Milk (page 36)!

SIBERIA CAKE

Time: 1 hour 30 minutes plus 24 hours resting time • **Yield:** 8 cake sandwich triangles

Siberia cake is composed of two thick slices of *castella* (pronounced "kasutera" in Japanese) sponge cake sandwiching a smooth layer of *mizu yōkan* red bean jelly. Siberia cake experienced its greatest popularity during the Meiji period (1868–1912 AD), but interest in the dish was revitalized by Hayao Miyazaki's film *The Wind Rises*.

CASTELLA CAKE

Nonstick cooking spray

5 large eggs, at room temperature

1 cup sugar

1²/₃ cups bread flour, sifted

5 tablespoons wildflower honey

2 tablespoons warm water

1 teaspoon vanilla extract

MIZU YŌKAN

1 cup water

1 teaspoon kanten powder

2 tablespoons sugar

1 pinch salt

1½ cups *koshi an* (smooth Red Bean Paste, page 12)

AS SEEN IN: *The Wind Rises*

In Hayao Miyazaki's *The Wind Rises*, engineer Jiro is commissioned to develop a military aircraft during the 1920s. This period of time in Japan was marked by widespread poverty, and in one poignant scene, Jiro offers Siberia cake to some hungry children, who end up running away before they can try the delicious treat. Don't make the same mistake that they did—whip up some delectable Siberia cake today!

TO MAKE THE CASTELLA CAKE:

1. Preheat your oven to 325°F.

2. Line two 8-by-8-by-2-inch baking pans with parchment paper, positioning the paper up the sides of the pans for easy cake removal, and apply a layer of nonstick cooking spray or butter to the paper.

3. In a stand mixer with a whisk attachment, whisk the eggs and the sugar on medium speed until the batter has a ribbon consistency, about 5 minutes. Gradually add the sifted bread flour in two stages while mixing to incorporate.

4. In a separate bowl, combine the honey, warm water, and vanilla extract. Add the honey mixture to the egg mixture and beat until an even batter forms, about 30 seconds.

5. Hold a mesh sieve over your cake pan and pour half of the batter mixture through the sieve. (You may want to weigh the total amount of batter to ensure your cakes are the same size.) Repeat with the second pan.

6. Smooth the tops of the cakes with a small offset spatula and bake for 40 minutes on your oven's middle rack, or until a toothpick comes out clean.

7. Pull the cakes out of the oven and let them cool for at least 20 minutes before removing them from the pans and transferring them to a wire rack.

TO MAKE THE MIZU YŌKAN:

1. In a medium saucepan over medium heat, combine the water and the kanten powder and bring it to a boil while whisking. Once the mixture is boiling, turn the heat down to low. Remove from heat after 2 minutes.

2. Add the sugar, salt, and *koshi an*, and continue mixing until they are completely incorporated and the mixture is smooth. Return the pan to medium heat and bring to a boil once more, then remove from heat.

3. Line a clean 8-by-8-inch pan with plastic wrap. Place one of your two *castella* cakes into the pan, golden side down. Pour the *mizu yōkan* over the *castella* cake and smooth it with an offset spatula. Then place the other *castella* cake on top of the *mizu yōkan*, golden side up. Cover the cake with plastic wrap and let it rest overnight in the refrigerator.

4. Remove the cake from the pan. Using a bread knife, cut the cake into four equal squares, and then cut each of those squares in half diagonally. Enjoy!

GIANT MANJU

Time: 1 hour 10 minutes • **Yield:** 2 large *manju* buns or 4 small *manju* buns

Manju are steamed buns typically filled with red bean paste or meat (the meaty version is called *nikuman*). The outer layer has a cake-like consistency, unlike the chewy texture of the mochi-covered *daifuku*. Using a steamer is crucial to the success of this recipe! (*Anpan* buns are very similar to *manju* but are baked instead of steamed.) While red bean paste is the most traditional *manju* filling, flavors vary from region to region in Japan, and *manju* can be found stuffed with cream, fruit, and other flavored bean fillings. Some even have an outer layer of flavored cake such as matcha or black sesame. Once you've mastered the red bean version of this recipe, level up and try the plum caramel version with white bean paste!

2¾ cups all-purpose flour, divided

4 teaspoons baking powder

¼ cup sugar

¾ cup water

1 cup Red Bean Paste (page 12), halved and chilled

Two 4-by-4-inch squares parchment paper, or four 3-by-3-inch squares for smaller buns

1. In a large bowl, whisk together 2½ cups of flour and baking powder. Add the sugar and whisk until evenly incorporated, then slowly add the water using a rubber spatula to stir. A shaggy dough will begin to form.

2. Sprinkle the remaining ¼ cup of flour on a clean work surface and place the dough on it. Knead the dough by hand for about 5 minutes. If the dough is dry, add an additional teaspoon of water.

3. Divide the dough into 2 equal pieces. Roll each piece into a ball, and then press it flat and roll it out until it is about ⅛ inch thick. For smaller buns, divide the dough into four equal pieces.

4. Place ½ of the Red Bean Paste on the center of each circle of dough, or ¼ of the Red Bean Paste for smaller buns. Wrap the dough around the bean paste and pinch the edges closed, then place the buns seam side down on a small square of parchment paper.

5. Place one bun and its parchment paper inside a steamer and steam for 19 minutes. (You will likely need to steam each of the buns separately due to their large size. If you make smaller buns, you will likely need to steam them two at a time in two batches.)

6. Enjoy while warm.

AS SEEN IN: *Spirited Away; Yona of the Dawn; Idolmaster*

In Hayao Miyazaki's *Spirited Away*, a kindly bathhouse worker takes pity on Chihiro and brings her a *manju* bun while she sits on a moonlit balcony contemplating her bleak situation. As big as Chihiro's head, this otherworldly *manju* is the epitome of comfort food. If being stranded in the spirit world while your parents have been transformed into pigs isn't a good enough reason to eat your feelings, I don't know what is!

PLUM CARAMEL MANJU

Time: 1 hour 30 minutes • **Yield:** 4 medium *manju* buns

DOUGH

2¾ cups all-purpose flour, divided

4 teaspoons baking powder

¼ cup sugar

¾ cup water

1 cup plum caramel bean paste, quartered and chilled

Four 2-by-2-inch squares parchment paper

PLUM CARAMEL BEAN PASTE

1¼ cups sugar

¾ cup water

⅓ cup plum wine (*umeshu*)

1 fresh plum, finely chopped

¾ cup White Bean Paste (page 13)

TO MAKE THE DOUGH:

1. In a large bowl, whisk together 2½ cups of flour and baking powder. Add the sugar and whisk until evenly incorporated, then slowly add the water using a rubber spatula to stir. A shaggy dough will begin to form.

2. Sprinkle the remaining ¼ cup of flour on a clean work surface and place the dough on it. Knead the dough by hand for about 5 minutes. If the dough is dry, add an additional teaspoon of water.

3. Divide the dough into 4 equal pieces.

TO MAKE THE PLUM CARAMEL BEAN PASTE:

1. In a medium saucepan over medium heat, whisk together the sugar and the water. Stir until the mixture begins to bubble and turn a golden color. Stop stirring and quickly take the caramel off the heat. Add the plum wine and chopped plum and stir until all lumps have dissolved.

2. Mix ¼ cup of the plum caramel sauce with the White Bean Paste. Refrigerate the mixture for at least 20 minutes. (Retain the excess plum caramel sauce as a topping for yogurt or ice cream.)

3. Once cool, place ¼ of the plum caramel bean paste on the center of each circle of dough. Wrap the dough around the bean paste and pinch the edges closed, then place the buns seam side down on a small square of parchment paper.

4. Place one bun and its parchment paper inside a steamer and steam for 17 minutes. (Due to their size, you will likely need to steam them in two separate batches of two.)

5. Enjoy while warm.

AS SEEN IN: *Shirobako; Little Busters!; Sweetness & Lightning*

In the first episode of *Shirobako*, a group of five girls create an anime for their school's cultural festival and vow to someday produce their own professional anime together. Meeting together for one of the last times as high schoolers, they chant, "Don-don-donuts, let's go nuts!" as they hoist their donuts in the air—a sugary toast to their bright future in anime production.

DON-DON-DONUTS

Time: 5 hours • **Yield:** Nine 4-inch donuts

Japan is known for its delicious chewy donuts. The ubiquitous chain Mister Donut (also called Misudo) popularized the pon-de-ring style of donut, which is composed of small balls of dough forming a ring. The chewy texture in Japan's donuts is achieved in a variety of ways—*mochiko* rice flour, tapioca flour, and silken tofu have all been used to create the effect. In this recipe, I utilize a mix of rice and bread flour and cut the dough with a donut cutter to achieve a similar shape to the one featured in *Shirobako*.

STARTER/YUDANE

1 cup *mochiko*

1 cup water

DONUTS

2 cups all-purpose flour, divided

1⅔ cups bread flour

1 large egg

1½ teaspoons instant dry yeast

1 teaspoon salt

3 tablespoons sugar

1 tablespoon unsalted butter, cubed

4 cups canola oil, or another oil without a strong flavor, for frying

½ teaspoon flaky sea salt

MISO CARAMEL SAUCE

1 cup sugar

6 tablespoons unsalted butter

½ cup heavy whipping cream

1 tablespoon white miso paste

TO MAKE THE STARTER:

1. Heat a small saucepan over medium heat. Add the *mochiko* and water and whisk steadily. When the ingredients start to stick together and form a blob (about 5 minutes), take the mixture off the heat and set aside.

TO MAKE THE DONUTS:

1. In a stand mixer with a dough hook attachment, combine the *mochiko* mixture with 1½ cups of all-purpose flour, bread flour, egg, instant dry yeast, salt, and sugar and mix on medium speed. The mixture should combine to form a dough that is moist to the touch.

3. Add the butter and continue to mix on medium speed for about 8 to 10 minutes. The dough should become elastic and stretchy.

4. Place the dough in a large greased bowl and cover with plastic wrap. Let it rest at room temperature for 3 hours. Once the dough has doubled in size, sprinkle the remaining ½ cup of all-purpose flour on a clean work surface and place the dough on it. Roll out the dough until it's about ½ inch thick.

5. Cut out donut shapes with a 4-inch donut cutter, then cut out a small square of parchment paper for each donut. Place each donut shape on a piece of parchment paper and cover the donuts with plastic wrap. Let them rest again for 1½ hours.

6. In a medium frying pan, heat the canola oil over medium heat. Once the oil temperature has reached 325°F, place two donuts in the pan, peeling off the parchment. Cook for 1 minute, flip with a spatula, and cook for 1 additional minute. Remove the donuts with tongs or a spider strainer and place on a cooling rack.

TO MAKE THE MISO CARAMEL SAUCE:

1. Pour the sugar into a medium saucepan and melt it over medium-high heat. Once most of it has melted (about 3 minutes), whisk a few times to remove any clumps. Once the sugar has all melted, continue cooking until it reaches the desired amber color, about 2 more minutes. Add the butter and whisk, then slowly add the heavy cream while constantly whisking until it is incorporated.

2. Remove the caramel sauce from heat and stir in the miso paste. Let the caramel sauce cool for about 10 minutes before applying it to your donuts with a spoon or offset spatula. Sprinkle the donuts with flaky sea salt before serving.

FROM THE
DAGASHIYA

DORAYAKI

Dorayaki is typically composed of two fluffy and moist pancakes sandwiching red bean paste, chestnuts, or cream. *Dorayaki* have been around since antiquity, but the modern round pancake shape was introduced during the Edo period (1603–1868 AD). Modern *dorayaki*, which are also influenced by the European *castella* cake, were introduced in 1914 by a shop called Usagiya in Ueno, Tokyo. To give them a little anime twist, here I'm including tie-dye and miniature *chibi* versions of this classic dessert.

AS SEEN IN: *Shōwa Genroku Rakugo Shinjū; Nisekoi; High School Fleet*

In Season 2 of *Shōwa Genroku Rakugo Shinjū*, one scene opens with Shinnosuke enjoying a fresh *dorayaki* pancake sandwich at a *rakugo* theater. *Rakugo* is a traditional Japanese art of comedic storytelling in which a lone performer sits on a cushion on a raised platform and tells humorous tales. The art form is still prominent in Japan and can be seen at specialty theaters called *yose*. Whether you're watching rakugo live at a theater or viewing an anime on your favorite streaming platform, *dorayaki* pancakes are a perfect companion snack.

TIE-DYE DORAYAKI

Time: 30 minutes • **Yield:** 6 pancake sandwiches

1 teaspoon pickled sakura blossoms

1 tablespoon wildflower honey

2 large eggs

2 teaspoons water

4 tablespoons sugar

½ teaspoon baking powder

½ cup all-purpose flour

2-4 drops pink gel food coloring

2-4 drops purple gel food coloring

2-4 drops blue gel food coloring

½ cup White Bean Paste (page 13)

1. Soak pickled sakura blossoms in a small bowl of water for 15 minutes to remove excess salt.

2. In a medium bowl, mix together the honey, eggs, water, and sugar. In a separate bowl, whisk together the baking powder and the flour. Then pour the dry ingredients into the wet ingredients and mix together. Let the batter rest for 5 minutes.

3. While waiting for the batter to rest, heat a large nonstick skillet over medium-low heat. Do not use butter or oil, as they can cause browning on your rainbow pancakes.

4. Divide your batter into three equal portions in three separate medium bowls. Add a different gel food coloring color to each bowl and mix until the color is evenly distributed.

5. Pour the colored batter from two of the bowls into the third bowl. Using a toothpick, gently swirl the colors together so that they intertwine but are still distinct.

6. Spoon 1 tablespoon of batter onto the skillet. Cook on medium-low heat for 30 seconds and flip to cook the other side. After another 30 seconds, remove from the skillet. Make 12 of these pancakes.

7. Pat the sakura blossoms dry with a paper towel, and then chop them and mix them with the White Bean Paste. Place this mixture in a small piping bag.

8. Pipe approximately ½ tablespoon of the bean paste mixture onto 6 of the pancakes using a round piping tip.

9. Place the remaining 6 pancakes onto each pancake topped with the bean paste, creating 6 pancake sandwiches.

CHIBI DORAYAKI

Time: 20 minutes
Yield: About 12 mini pancake sandwiches

1 tablespoon wildflower honey

2 large eggs

2 teaspoons water

4 tablespoons sugar

½ teaspoon baking powder

½ cup all-purpose flour

Black sesame seeds for garnishing

¾ cup *koshi an* (smooth Red Bean Paste, page 12)

1. In a medium bowl, mix together the honey, eggs, water, and sugar. In a separate bowl, whisk together the baking powder and the flour. Then pour the dry ingredients into the wet ingredients and mix together. Let the batter rest for 5 minutes.

2. While waiting for the batter to rest, heat a large nonstick skillet over medium-low heat. Using a ½-tablespoon scoop, dollop four separate scoops of batter onto your skillet, spaced so that their edges don't touch. Quickly sprinkle the top of each pancake with a small pinch of black sesame seeds to taste.

3. Cook until golden, about 30 seconds. When the pancakes are ready, you will notice small bubbles forming on the surface. Flip the pancakes and cook on the other side for another 30 seconds. Take pancakes off the heat and let cool. Repeat with the remaining batter. Make 24 pancakes.

4. Fill a small piping bag with *koshi an*, and pipe a generous portion of the bean paste onto 12 of the pancakes using a round piping tip.

5. Place the remaining 12 pancakes onto each pancake topped with bean paste, creating 12 mini pancake sandwiches.

WARABI MOCHI

Time: 1 hour 30 minutes
Yield: Twenty-five 1-by-1-inch warabi mochi cubes

Warabi mochi is a summer *wagashi* made from bracken starch (warabi *mochiko*) instead of rice flour (*mochiko*), and its texture is slightly different from rice-based mochi. The warabi mochi itself isn't strongly flavored, but it carries the flavor of its toppings. Warabi mochi is typically topped with *kinako* (soybean powder). If you can't find warabi *mochiko* for this recipe, you can substitute tapioca flour, but this will alter the texture. Warabi mochi is often served with *kuromitsu* syrup, which can be purchased or made by heating equal parts dark brown sugar or *kurozato* (Okinawan black sugar) and water over low heat.

½ cup *kinako,* divided

¾ cup warabi *mochiko*

1½ cups water

½ cup sugar

1. Prepare an 8-by-8-inch cake pan by sprinkling it with ⅛ cup of *kinako* flour.

2. In a medium saucepan, mix the warabi *mochiko*, water, and sugar together until the ingredients have dissolved and are evenly incorporated. Heat the pan over medium heat and stir with a whisk for 10 minutes, until the mixture thickens.

3. Quickly pour the batter into the prepared cake pan while the mixture is still hot.

4. Sprinkle with ⅓ cup of *kinako* and refrigerate for at least 30 minutes.

5. Cut the mochi into cubes with a sharp knife and toss the cubes in the remaining *kinako* flour. Serve chilled.

AS SEEN IN: *Let's Make a Mug Too; Rokuhōdō Yotsuiro Biyori*

In episode 8 of the slice-of-life anime *Let's Make a Mug Too*, Koizumi Mami brings some wobbly warabi mochi to Aoki Tōko, who is busy on her pottery wheel. Pottery pairs wonderfully with this traditional *wagashi*—pick a special dish from your collection when plating your toothsome warabi mochi!

ANMITSU

Time: 30 minutes plus 1 hour refrigeration • **Yield:** 3 bowls

Anmitsu is traditionally served in teahouses and specialty cafés. It typically features kanten jelly, *dango*, fresh cut fruit, red bean paste, and black sugar syrup, and it often includes a scoop of ice cream as well. It's meant to be a cooling dessert enjoyed during the summer, with the chewy texture of the kanten jelly complementing the hearty and rich texture of the red bean paste.

KANTEN JELLY

Nonstick cooking spray

3 tablespoons kanten powder

2¼ cups water

6 tablespoons sugar

6 drops flavor extract (optional)

KUROMITSU SYRUP

½ cup water

½ cup sugar

½ cup dark brown sugar

ANMITSU

6 *Dango* Dumplings (pages 37–38)

1½ cups sliced fruit (such as kiwis, bananas, mandarin oranges, blueberries)

6 tablespoons *tsubu an* (coarse Red Bean Paste, page 12)

3 small scoops matcha ice cream

3 maraschino cherries

AS SEEN IN: *Kantai Collection; Fuuka; Recovery of an MMO Junkie*

Kantai Collection features a group of girls who are inhabited by the spirits of historical naval vessels. In episode 3, Fubuki's squadron is tasked with luring the enemy out at night. Fubuki is nervous and concerned, and her friends try to boost her morale at a café where she is given a brimming bowl of *anmitsu* on the house. A bowl of *anmitsu* will do the trick when you need a confidence boost!

TO MAKE THE KANTEN JELLY:

1. Prepare an 8-by-8-inch heatproof glass baking dish by spraying it with a small amount of nonstick cooking spray and then wiping it down with a small piece of paper towel.

2. In a medium saucepan over medium heat, add the kanten powder to the water and let it dissolve for 5 minutes. Bring the mixture to a simmer while whisking constantly. Add the sugar and continue to stir for 3 minutes.

3. Take the mixture off the heat and add your preferred flavor extract, then pour the mixture into the prepared baking dish. Refrigerate for at least 1 hour, or until firm.

4. Once firm, remove the kanten jelly from the pan and place it on a cutting board. Cut it first into long strips and then into cubes. Retain 1½ cups of the cubes for the *anmitsu* and store the rest in the refrigerator.

TO MAKE THE KUROMITSU SYRUP:

1. Combine water, sugar, and dark brown sugar in a medium pan over medium-low heat. Bring to a simmer and cook for 20 minutes, stirring occasionally. Remove the syrup from the heat and let cool for 10 minutes.

TO MAKE THE ANMITSU:

1. Divide the kanten jelly cubes equally between the three serving bowls, then arrange *Dango* and sliced fruit on top of the jelly so that all the ingredients are visible.

2. Add 2 tablespoons of *tsubu an* and 1 scoop of matcha ice cream to each bowl. Pour *kuromitsu* syrup on top of each dish and garnish each bowl with a maraschino cherry.

RAINBOW CRYSTAL KOHAKUTOU

Time: 2 hours 25 minutes, plus 2 days drying • **Yield:** 30 to 50 crystal candies

AS SEEN IN: *Land of the Lustrous; Sailor Moon*

Land of the Lustrous is set far in the future, long after humans have gone extinct. Their descendants, living gemstones known as the Lustrous, roam the Earth while defending themselves from the Lunarians, who hunt the Lustrous to wear them as decorations. You can contemplate this strangely beautiful dystopian vision while enjoying these edible versions of its cast of characters!

Kohakutou are gemlike *wagashi* with a crunchy exterior and a smooth interior. Dye them to resemble the many colors of the Lustrous and admire their beauty—luckily, shattering and eating these lovely candies won't have any negative consequences!

1 tablespoon kanten or agar agar powder

¾ cup plus 1 tablespoon water

1⅔ cups sugar

4 drops flavor extract of your choice (I recommend mango and green apple)

Nonstick cooking spray

3 to 4 drops gel food coloring of your choice

Edible silver paint for garnishing (optional)

1. In a medium saucepan over medium heat, add the kanten powder to the water and let it dissolve for 5 minutes. Bring the mixture to a simmer while whisking constantly. Add the sugar and continue to stir for 3 minutes.

2. Remove from heat, add the flavor extract, and stir to combine.

3. Spray an 8-by-11-inch heatproof glass baking dish with a small amount of flavorless nonstick cooking spray and spread it with a small piece of paper towel. Pour the kanten mixture into the dish.

4. Add the food coloring drops and use a toothpick to swirl and distribute the color, then chill for at least 2 hours in the refrigerator.

5. Use a sharp knife to cut the chilled mixture into strips, then cut the strips down into your preferred diamond shapes.

6. Line a sheet pan with wax or parchment paper. Place the crystals on the pan and let them dry, covered with plastic wrap, at room temperature for 2 days.

7. After drying, as an optional finishing touch, use a food-safe paintbrush to paint the *kohakutou* crystal edges with edible silver paint to add a special crystal dimension.

IE NI
AT HOME

HOT HONEY MILK

Time: 10 minutes • **Yield**: 1 mug

This mug of liquid comfort will transport you back to a simpler time. In this recipe, I recommend topping the soul-warming beverage with cinnamon, *kinako* powder, or matcha powder to amp up the soothing flavor. Drink it when you need a rainy day pick-me-up, before you go to bed, or any other time when you need a dose of relaxation.

1 cup whole milk or milk of choice

1 tablespoon honey

1 teaspoon ground cinnamon, *kinako* powder, or matcha powder

1. Warm your milk on the stove in a medium saucepan over medium-low heat.

2. Whisk in honey until combined and continue to heat the mixture to your desired temperature. Take the pan off the heat after it has started simmering but just before it begins to boil, about 5 minutes.

3. Pour the contents into a favorite mug but not all the way to the top. Then, using a milk frother, froth the milk until a layer of bubbles appears, about 30 seconds.

4. Sprinkle a pinch of cinnamon, *kinako* powder, or matcha powder into your mug to taste. (You may want to use a fine mesh sieve to distribute evenly.) Enjoy immediately!

AS SEEN IN: *Ponyo; Yuri Kuma Arashi; Black Butler*

In Hayao Miyazaki's *Ponyo*, a small fish named Ponyo turns into a human girl out of love for Sosuke, a five-year-old boy. Her extraordinary transformation upsets the balance of the sea and causes a gale of hurricane intensity. Once the two children are safe at Sosuke's home after being caught up in the magical storm, his mother makes them some hot milk and honey to help them warm up.

OHAGI

Time: 1 hour 30 minutes • **Yield:** 8 pieces

Ohagi are balls of lightly mashed glutinous and nonglutinous rice covered with red bean paste. *Ohagi* are primarily enjoyed during the autumn, while *botamochi* (another word for *ohagi*) are enjoyed during the spring; both are associated with *higan*, the Buddhist holidays that are celebrated in Japan during the equinoxes. The main difference between *ohagi* and *botamochi* is the type of bean paste used. In autumn, the red beans are freshly harvested and tender, so the skin of the beans is included in the paste (*tsubu an*). In spring, the beans have overwintered and hardened, so the skin is removed (*koshi an*).

2½ cups glutinous rice (*mochigome*)

½ cup sushi rice

3 cups water

3 cups *tsubu an* (coarse Red Bean Paste, page 12)

1 tablespoon matcha powder

1. Rinse the rice in a colander. Once rinsed and drained, set aside for 30 minutes. Place the rice in a rice cooker and fill with 3 cups of water. Let the rice sit in the water for an additional 30 minutes before cooking.

2. Cook the rice, then let it cool, uncovered, for 30 minutes.

3. Using a large spoon or pestle, lightly smash the rice until it gains a sticky consistency but is not completely mashed or smooth. Form the rice into balls, about 2 tablespoons each.

4. Gently cover each rice ball with about ⅓ cup of the *tsubu an*. Using a fine mesh sieve, sift matcha powder on top of each piece of *ohagi* before serving.

AS SEEN IN: *Twin Star Exorcists; The Helpful Fox Senko-san; Someday's Dreamers*

In episode 29 of *Twin Star Exorcists*, Sae shows Benio her drawings of the "*Ohagi* Man" as they travel to Benio's hometown of Kyoto. Benio recommends Kinkakuji, the Golden Pavilion, as a sightseeing destination, but his true goal is revealed to be an *ohagi* shop near the temple that serves the best *ohagi* in the city. While a visit to Kinkakuji is always worthwhile, you can make *ohagi* at home to snack on while you get your travel plans in order.

JAPANESE-STYLE HOTCAKES

Time: 45 minutes • **Yield:** 4 medium hotcakes

Japanese-style hotcakes are known for their fluffy, soufflé-like consistency. This is achieved by separating out the egg yolks and whipping the whites into a meringue, as well as adding a bit of water to the pan to mimic the effects of a steamer. Japanese hotcakes tend to be lighter and less sweet than other types of pancakes—which of course means that you can eat more of them!

2 large eggs, yolks and
   whites separated

2 tablespoons sugar

½ teaspoon cream of tartar

¼ cup cake flour

½ teaspoon baking powder

1½ tablespoons whole milk

½ teaspoon vanilla or almond extract

1 tablespoon vegetable oil

1 tablespoon water

3 tablespoons salted butter,
   at room temperature

1 teaspoon wildflower honey

½ teaspoon white miso

¼ cup pure maple syrup

1. In a stand mixer, whip egg whites on high until frothy, about 1 minute, to create a meringue. Add sugar and cream of tartar and continue to whip on the highest setting until soft peaks form and your meringue is glossy, about 5 minutes.

2. In a separate bowl, whisk the flour, baking powder, whole milk, egg yolks, and almond extract together until combined.

3. Heat a large frying pan over low heat and add the vegetable oil to the pan. It's important to keep the heat low and even.

4. Add a spoonful of meringue to your yolk mixture and mix to combine. Then slowly fold the rest of the meringue mixture into the yolk mixture using a rubber spatula, folding in the same direction. Work slowly to prevent the structure from deflating.

5. Fill a piping bag with pancake batter. Using a round tip, pipe ¼ of the pancake mixture into the hot frying pan. Pile the batter high instead of wide to build up the hotcake's structure. Cover the pan with a lid and cook for 1 minute.

6. Add an extra, smaller spoonful of batter on top of your hotcake. Cook for 2 more minutes with the lid on.

7. Using a slotted spatula, flip the hotcake. Then add a few drops of water around the hotcake and put the lid back on. Cook for an additional 4 minutes before removing from heat. Repeat the process for the remaining hotcakes.

8. Using a whisk, mix the butter with the honey and miso in a small bowl until smooth. Top the hotcakes with a generous amount of the honey butter and maple syrup to taste.

AS SEEN IN: *Space Brothers; Hi Score Girl; Is the Order a Rabbit?*

In episode 16 of *Space Brothers*, prospective astronaut Serika Itō makes hotcakes for his fellow trainees at the Japanese Aerospace Exploration Agency. However, he is forced to serve smaller portions than usual, because they still have four days left to go on their simulated space journey and supplies are starting to run low. Whether you're sealed inside a closed testing environment built to mimic a spaceship or not, I guarantee that you won't want to ration these delicious treats!

FUA FUA FRENCH TOAST

Time: 25 minutes plus soaking time overnight • **Yield**: 4 triangles of thick French toast

Japanese French toast gets its custard-like consistency from soaking thick *shokupan* bread slices in batter overnight. The longer you let the bread absorb the liquids, the more of a custardy quality your French toast will have!

¼ cup all-purpose flour

3 large eggs

½ cup whole milk

1 teaspoon vanilla extract

Two 2-inch slices *Shokupan* bread (page 54)

1 tablespoon ground cinnamon

1 tablespoon sugar

1 tablespoon vegetable oil

1 banana, peeled and sliced or cut into shapes with a cookie cutter

1 tablespoon chocolate sauce

1 sprig fresh mint

1. In a large bowl, whisk together the flour, eggs, milk, and vanilla extract.

2. Using a bread knife, remove the crusts and cut each slice of *Shokupan* diagonally to form two triangles.

3. Submerge the bread slices in the egg mixture and let them soak in a sealed container for at least 15 minutes, but ideally for 12 hours.

4. Mix the cinnamon and sugar together in a small bowl.

5. Heat the vegetable oil in a large frying pan over medium-low heat and place two pieces of bread in the pan. Cover with a lid and cook until golden brown, about 5 minutes. Flip the bread with a pair of kitchen tongs and cook for an additional 3 minutes. Repeat the process with the remaining two pieces.

6. Plate your French toast on a large plate. Using a mesh sieve, sift all of your cinnamon sugar mixture over it. Arrange your banana slices on the side of the plate and drizzle chocolate sauce over the toast. Garnish with fresh mint.

AS SEEN IN: *Encouragement of Climb; Selector Infected WIXOSS; Wataten: An Angel Flew Down to Me*

Encouragement of Climb follows shy Ao Kimura as she overcomes her fear of the outdoors and climbing with the help of some nature-loving friends. During a sleepover in episode 11, Aoi and Kokona plan a special dish for their upcoming outing to Hanno River Beach. With fluffy French toast on the menu, this trip is sure to be a success. Follow the girls' lead and whip up some French toast to fuel your next adventure!

HISHI MOCHI

Time: 1 hour • **Yield:** About 16 diamond pieces

Hishi mochi features the same beautiful springtime colors as *Hanami Dango* (page 37)—*hishi* refers to their diamond shape, which traditionally represents fertility in Japan. This special *wagashi* is closely associated with Hinamatsuri, the Festival of Dolls (also known as Girls' Day), which falls on March 3 in Japan. Hina dolls are meant to cleanse children of sickness and are traditionally placed near a child's pillow until they are three years old.

½ cup potato starch for dusting

3 cups *mochiko*, divided

3 cups sugar, divided

3 cups water, divided

1 tablespoon matcha powder

1 drop pink gel food coloring

AS SEEN IN: *Shirokuma Cafe; K-On!!; Recorder and Randsell*

In episode 46 of *Shirokuma Cafe*, the café's polar bear owner surprises his group of friends with a gift of multicolored *hishi* mochi. Watching these animal friends enjoy this seasonal treat will surely put you in the mood to make this recipe!

1. Prepare an 8-by-8-inch baking pan by dusting it with a generous amount of potato starch.

2. In a large heatproof mixing bowl, whisk together 1 cup each of the *mochiko*, sugar, and water. Add the matcha powder and mix to combine; this will make the green layer of mochi.

3. Cover the bowl with plastic wrap and microwave for 2 minutes on medium heat. The mixture should start to bubble. Stir the mixture, then re-cover with the plastic wrap and microwave for an additional 2 minutes. Remove and stir with a rubber spatula. The mochi should no longer be a liquid but should still have a spreadable, stretchy consistency.

4. Prepare a clean work surface and dust with potato starch. Transfer the mochi from the bowl to the work surface and roll out the green matcha layer with a plastic rolling pin, then stretch it to fill the inside of your prepared pan. Lightly dust with potato starch and pat down to form an even layer.

5. Repeat steps 2 through 4 above for the white and the pink layers, adding a drop of pink gel food coloring to the pink layer mixture before microwaving. Place the white layer on top of the green layer in the pan, followed by the pink layer.

6. Dust the top of the pink layer with potato starch and pat it down to make an even surface. Cover the mochi with plastic wrap and refrigerate it for 30 minutes.

7. Using a diamond-shaped cookie cutter or a sharp knife, cut your mochi into diamond shapes about 3 inches long.

8. Enjoy with a cup of hot matcha!

CHEESE MUFFINS

Time: 45 minutes • **Yield:** 6 large muffins

AS SEEN IN: *Hakkenden: Eight Dogs of the East*

Hamaji requests that Sosuke Inukawa make some muffins in episode 9 of *Hakkenden: Eight Dogs of the East*. The resulting muffins—some blueberry, some walnut, and some flavored with cheese—radiate sugary glory as Sosuke presents them, but it's the cheese muffins that really steal the show. Recreate their eye-catching sparkle with some edible glitter!

For this recipe, I use mild white cheddar cut into cubes so that the muffins appear as similar as possible to Sosuke's, but feel free to use shredded cheese as a substitute to obtain a more widespread and less concentrated cheese flavor.

Nonstick cooking spray

6 tablespoons unsalted butter, melted and cooled to room temperature

1 tablespoon sugar

1 cup whole milk

1 large egg

2 cups all-purpose flour

1 tablespoon baking powder

1 teaspoon salt

1 cup white cheddar cheese, cut into ½-inch cubes and divided into two portions

1 pinch silver edible glitter

1. Preheat your oven to 350°F.

2. Line a large muffin tin with muffin liners, or grease with nonstick cooking spray.

3. In a stand mixer with a paddle attachment, mix together the butter, sugar, and milk on medium speed. Add the egg and whisk to combine.

4. In a separate large bowl, combine the flour, baking powder, and salt and whisk until combined. In three additions, fold the wet ingredients into the dry ingredients in the large bowl. Add ½ cup of the cheddar cheese cubes and stir until evenly distributed.

5. Scoop the batter into muffin holders until each is ½ to ¾ full, then place the remaining ½ cup of cheddar cheese cubes onto the tops of the muffins.

6. Bake for 25 minutes, or until a toothpick comes out clean. Sprinkle a pinch of edible glitter onto the finished muffins, and enjoy while warm!

STEAMED CINNAMON RAISIN MUFFINS

Time: 1 hour 15 minutes • **Yield:** 1 dozen muffins

AS SEEN IN: *Anohana: The Flower We Saw That Day*

In *Anohana: The Flower We Saw That Day*, Jintan can't escape the ghostly chattering of Menma, a childhood friend who died years ago and whom no one else can see. Menma had a wish that only Jintan can fulfill, but she can't remember what it was! In episode 3, she remembers that Jintan's mother used to make cinnamon raisin muffins for all their friends before she herself passed away. Menma takes it upon herself to try to replicate these muffins, hoping this might remind her of her wish. Try them yourself and see what memories they might evoke in you!

Menma cooks these muffins in a steamer. In our recipe, I recommend using a steamer as well, but if you don't have access to one, you can use a double boiler over the stove to achieve the same effect.

2¼ cups all-purpose flour

½ cup sugar

1 tablespoon baking powder

½ teaspoon sea salt

1 teaspoon ground cinnamon

1 large egg

1 cup whole milk

¼ cup unsalted butter, melted and cooled to room temperature

½ cup raisins

2 tablespoons turbinado sugar or 1 cup *koshi an* (smooth Red Bean Paste, page 12)

1. Gather 12 standard foil muffin liners.

2. Combine all the dry ingredients except the turbinado sugar in a large mixing bowl and whisk to combine.

3. Whisk the egg and milk in a separate bowl until combined, then whisk the liquid butter into the mixture. Gradually fold the wet mixture into the bowl of dry ingredients until combined.

4. Add the raisins to the batter and mix until they are evenly distributed.

5. Create a double boiler on your stovetop by placing a medium saucepan half filled with water underneath a larger empty pot with a lid. The bottom of the pot should not be in contact with the water below it.

6. Fill each muffin liner ¾ full with batter, about 2 tablespoons each. Sprinkle the top of each muffin with turbinado sugar. Alternatively, pipe a spiral of *koshi an* bean paste on top of your muffins. (You can buy store-bought *koshi an* in a squeezable tube that's perfect for this.)

7. Place 6 of your muffins in the steamer. If using a double boiler, wrap the pot's lid in a kitchen towel before placing it on the pot. This will prevent condensation from the steam from dripping onto your muffins.

8. Over medium heat, steam your muffins for 32 minutes, or until a toothpick comes out clean. The muffins will fill the entire pan and may not be perfectly round, which is expected. Carefully remove each muffin using a long serving spoon to prevent burning yourself in the steam. Repeat until the remaining batter is gone.

MINI HERRING AND PUMPKIN POTPIES

Time: 2 hours 20 minutes • **Yield:** 6 mini potpies

The pies in this recipe are individually portioned in ramekins, perfect for a dinner party course or a snack. The recipe uses kabocha, a variety of Japanese pumpkin with a green skin that is a popular autumn flavor in Japan. Herring, a staple food in Sweden (where *Kiki's Delivery Service* is set), was widely harvested in Hokkaido until the 1950s, when overfishing caused a decline in the natural population. Although it was traditionally a harbinger of spring, herring and many other varieties of fish are now available year-round thanks to commercial aquaculture. Feel free to use store-bought puff pastry for this recipe to cut down on preparation time.

AS SEEN IN: *Kiki's Delivery Service*

In Hayao Miyazaki's *Kiki's Delivery Service*, Kiki has to deliver a herring and pumpkin potpie before she can go to a party. When she arrives to pick up the pie, however, she discovers that it hasn't even been baked yet, and in the chaos that ensues, she manages to miss the party and then temporarily loses her powers as a witch. But even though it brought Kiki bad luck, you should still give this savory treat a chance!

PUFF PASTRY

1 cup all-purpose flour

1 pinch salt

10 tablespoons unsalted butter, cubed and chilled

1/3 cup ice water

KABOCHA PURÉE

1 cup drained canned smoked herring (roughly 3 fillets per ramekin)

1/2 kabocha squash

4 tablespoons unsalted butter

1/4 cup packed dark brown sugar

1/2 cup white onion, diced

1 teaspoon garlic powder

1/2 teaspoon salt

1/2 teaspoon ground black pepper

BÉCHAMEL SAUCE

2 cups whole milk

6 tablespoons unsalted butter

4 tablespoons all-purpose flour

1 pinch salt

1/4 cup finely grated Parmesan cheese

EGG WASH

1 large egg yolk

1/4 cup whole milk

1/4 cup canned black olives, sliced, for garnishing

(Continued on next page)

**TO MAKE THE PUFF PASTRY
(THIS STEP CAN BE DONE A DAY AHEAD):**

1. Combine the flour and salt in a medium bowl and stir. Using your hands, work the cubed butter into the flour until it is composed of pea-sized pieces of dough. Add the ice water and knead to combine.

2. Continue to knead the dough on a floured surface. Roll out the dough and fold it in thirds. Repeat 5 times. Then wrap your rectangle of dough in plastic wrap and refrigerate it for at least 1 hour.

TO MAKE THE KABOCHA PURÉE:

1. Preheat your oven to 375°F and line six 3½-inch-wide ramekins with 3 herring fillets in each ramekin.

2. Cut the squash in half lengthwise and wrap each half in foil. Place the wrapped kabocha halves on a small sheet pan and roast on the middle rack of the oven for 15 minutes.

3. Remove the kabocha from the oven and allow it to cool for 15 minutes. Then remove the skin and seeds and cut the squash into 1-inch cubes.

4. In a small saucepan over medium heat, warm the butter until it begins to brown, about 5 minutes. Remove from heat.

5. Combine the roast kabocha, dark brown sugar, and browned butter in a food processor and pulse on medium speed until smooth, about 30 seconds. Then add the onion, garlic powder, salt, and pepper, and pulse until incorporated, about 15 seconds.

6. Spoon an even amount (about 2 tablespoons) of the kabocha purée into each ramekin, on top of the herring.

TO MAKE THE BÉCHAMEL SAUCE:

1. Warm the milk in a small saucepan over medium heat until it is simmering but not boiling. Heat the butter in a separate small saucepan over medium heat until it has melted but not browned, about 2 minutes. (You can also melt the butter in a microwave oven.) Take the melted butter off the heat.

2. Add the flour and salt to the melted butter and stir with a wooden spoon, then return the butter and flour mixture to the stove. Cook on medium-low heat for about 5 minutes. The mix will appear more golden in color but not browned.

3. Add the heated milk to the flour mixture in small increments, whisking constantly over low heat. Cook until bubbling, about 5 minutes. Take off the heat and stir in the Parmesan cheese.

4. Evenly distribute the béchamel sauce into each ramekin.

5. Roll out the puff pastry dough with a rolling pin. Cut into 6 equal squares and drape the squares over the tops of the ramekins. Press the edges of the dough along the sides of the ramekins and trim off any excess with pastry scissors.

6. Roll out the leftover dough and cut out fish or pumpkin shapes with a small cookie cutter. Place the shapes on top of each ramekin. Feel free to get creative with your puff pastry design!

TO MAKE THE EGG WASH:

1. Mix the egg yolk and whole milk in a small bowl. Brush the top of each ramekin with the egg wash and arrange the sliced olives around the outer rim of each ramekin.

2. Bake for 15 minutes on the oven's middle rack, or until the puff pastry has turned a golden brown color.

SATA ANDAGI OKINAWAN DONUTS

Time: 45 minutes • **Yield:** 18 donuts

Sata andagi are deep-fried donuts with a crunchy exterior and a soft interior. They are traditionally made with cake flour, sugar, and eggs and are typically a bit denser than Western-style donuts. The dish traveled from Okinawa to Hawaii, where milk and vanilla were added to the recipe to create a softer crumb texture. Be sure to try them when they're warm and fresh! *Sata andagi* are typically made at home, but you can sometimes find them at festivals or at-home-style eateries in Okinawa. They keep for about 2 days when refrigerated. Reheat them by baking them in the oven for 8 minutes at 350°F.

5 cups plus 1 tablespoon vegetable oil

2 cups cake flour or all-purpose flour

2 teaspoons baking powder

1 large pinch salt

1 cup sugar

3 tablespoons evaporated milk

$\frac{1}{3}$ cup water

2 large eggs

1. Prepare a large stainless steel pan or wok for frying. Heat 5 cups vegetable oil over high heat, until it reaches 330°F.

2. In a medium bowl, whisk together the cake flour, baking powder, salt, and sugar. In a separate medium bowl, combine the evaporated milk, water, eggs, and the remaining 1 tablespoon vegetable oil.

3. Add $\frac{1}{3}$ of your wet ingredients to your dry ingredients bowl, and gently fold in with a rubber spatula as a dough begins to form. Add the rest of your wet ingredients in two stages, gently folding them in.

4. Form ping-pong-ball-sized dough balls, using a cup or small plate containing 1 tablespoon of vegetable oil at the side of your workstation to wet your hands so that the dough doesn't stick to them.

5. Drop the dough balls into the oil in two batches, being careful not to overcrowd them so they don't stick together. Fry for 8 minutes, or until the dough has achieved a golden brown color.

6. Remove the *sata andagi* from the oil with a mesh sieve or slotted spoon, and enjoy immediately!

AS SEEN IN: *The Aquatope on White Sand; Azumanga Daioh*

After giving up her dream of becoming a J-pop idol in *The Aquatope on White Sand*, Fūka Miyazawa leaves Tokyo and travels to Okinawa, where she meets Kukuru Misakino, the interim director at the Gama Gama Aquarium. Kukuru's grandparents feed her *sata andagi*, and Fūka quickly decides to stay in Okinawa and work at the aquarium as well. Take a mental vacation to that beautiful island with these bite-sized donuts!

AS SEEN IN: *The Way of the Househusband*

When Tatsu's wife, Miku, tries to surprise him with a birthday cake in episode 5 of *The Way of the Househusband*, she winds up making a huge mess in the kitchen that Tatsu has to clean up. Relatable! But because Miku worked so hard, Tatsu decides to salvage the cake, and the results are both beautiful and delicious.

BIRTHDAY CAKE

Time: 1 hour 20 minutes • **Yield:** 2 plated desserts

In this recipe, you'll recreate a loaf cake that mimics the slices on Tatsu's and Miku's plates. And while you can bake this cake from scratch, feel free to try reclaiming one of your own significant other's less-than-perfect creations and turn it into a work of art with an irresistible garnish!

CAKE

Nonstick cooking spray

1½ cups cake flour

1 teaspoon baking powder

¼ teaspoon baking soda

1 large pinch salt

¼ cup sour cream

½ cup whole milk

½ cup unsalted butter, at room temperature

1 cup sugar

3 large egg whites

2 teaspoons vanilla extract

2 slices honeydew melon or Galia melon

4 strawberries, hulled and thinly sliced

Fresh mint for garnishing

6 candles for garnishing

BUTTERCREAM

½ cup unsalted butter, at room temperature

2 cups powdered sugar

2 teaspoons vanilla extract

1 large pinch salt

2 tablespoons heavy whipping cream

WHIPPED CREAM

½ cup heavy whipping cream

1 tablespoon sugar

½ teaspoon vanilla extract

TO MAKE THE CAKE:

1. Line a 9-by-5-by-2½-inch loaf pan with parchment paper and spray with nonstick cooking spray.

2. Preheat your oven to 350°F.

3. In a medium bowl, sift the flour and add the baking powder, baking soda, and salt, whisking to combine. In a separate small bowl, mix together the sour cream and the milk.

4. In a stand mixer with a paddle attachment, beat the butter on a medium speed until it is light and fluffy. Add the sugar and mix until combined, then add the egg whites and the vanilla extract and continue to beat until they are incorporated.

5. Add the flour mixture and the sour cream mixture to the stand mixer bowl in three stages, alternating between the wet and dry components, and mix until incorporated.

6. Pour the resulting batter into your loaf pan. Bake for 40 minutes, or until a toothpick comes out clean.

TO MAKE THE BUTTERCREAM:

1. While the cake is baking, in a stand mixer with a paddle attachment, beat the butter on high speed until it is light and fluffy. Add the powdered sugar in three stages on low speed, then add the vanilla, salt, and heavy whipping cream and beat to combine.

2. Remove the cake from the oven and let it cool for 15 minutes before removing it from the pan. Once the cake has cooled, apply a thick layer of buttercream to the top of the cake with an offset spatula.

TO MAKE THE WHIPPED CREAM:

1. Using a chilled bowl, whip heavy whipping cream with a stand mixer for 1 minute on high speed. Add the sugar and the vanilla extract and continue to whip until soft peaks form.

2. Cut cake into 6 equal slices. On each of 2 large plates, place 3 slices of cake stacked like toppled dominoes. Add 1 slice of melon to the side of each plate, along with the sliced strawberries arranged in a fan pattern.

3. Fill a piping bag with the whipped cream and pipe the whipped cream onto the cake slices using a large star tip. Garnish with sprigs of mint.

4. Add 3 candles per plated dessert to achieve the same look as Tatsu's plated birthday cake!

ISSHO NI
TO SHARE

THE PERFECT PARFAIT, TWO WAYS

Parfaits in Japan come in countless varieties, and they often showcase seasonal fruits, ice cream, whipped cream, and cookies. They are usually intended for two or more people, and some shops even serve extra-large parfaits for big groups. The following recipes are intended to be made in large sundae glasses and are perfect for splitting with a fellow anime lover!

AS SEEN IN: *3D Kanojo; Gintama; Rainy Cocoa*

In *3D Kanojo*, Hikari Tsutsui sits with Arisa Ishino, who eats a parfait as they discuss ways for Hikari to express his feelings to Iroha Igarashi. It is an impressive parfait, featuring a full *purin*, various fruits, vanilla ice cream, and a granola mix. Arisa even orders a second parfait before leaving. These desserts are meant to be extravagant, so follow your heart when it comes to picking your ingredients!

KAWAII PARFAIT

Time: 10 minutes • **Yield:** 1 large (16-ounce) parfait

CHOCOLATE WHIPPED CREAM

½ cup heavy whipping cream

1 tablespoon sugar

1 tablespoon cocoa powder

PARFAIT

1 cup raspberries, or another red fruit of your choice

1½ cups chocolate cereal

1 cup Chocolate Cream (page 60)

1 scoop chocolate ice cream

1 scoop strawberry or cherry ice cream

½ cup Koala's March cookies

3 fresh strawberries, sliced and cut into shapes with a small flower cookie cutter

TO MAKE THE CHOCOLATE WHIPPED CREAM:

1. Using a chilled bowl, whip heavy whipping cream in a stand mixer on medium speed for 30 seconds. Add the sugar and cocoa powder and continue to whip until stiff peaks form.

TO MAKE THE PARFAIT:

1. Add ½ cup of raspberries to the bottom of a large sundae dish and pack down. Cover the raspberries with ¾ cup of chocolate cereal and add ½ cup of chocolate cream.

2. Repeat step 2. Ingredients should stack close to the height of your glass. Top with chocolate ice cream and strawberry ice cream.

3. Using a piping bag with a large star tip, pipe on the chocolate whipped cream and garnish with Koala's March cookies and fresh strawberry cutouts.

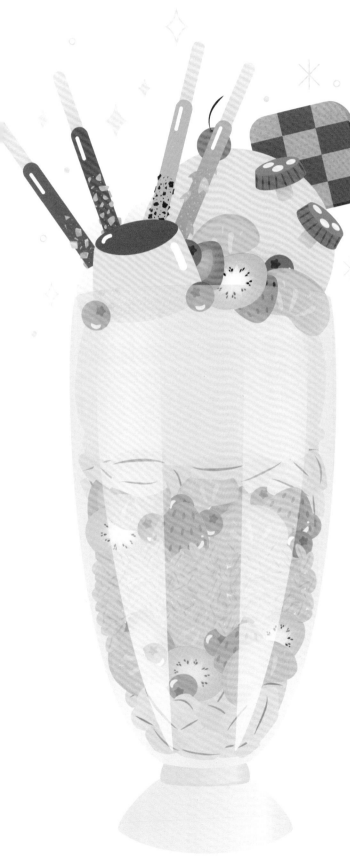

CRAZY PARFAIT

Time: 10 minutes • **Yield:** 1 large (16-ounce) parfait

1 cup chopped Milano milk chocolate cookies

1 cup sliced mixed fruit (such as orange, kiwi, banana, and strawberry)

½ cup granola, in preferred flavor

1 scoop vanilla ice cream

1 scoop caramel ice cream

1 *Purin* (page 33)

3 Apricot Yuzu Marshmallows (page 101)

1 maraschino cherry

1 *Chibi Dorayaki* (page 72)

1. Add ½ cup of chopped Milano cookies to the bottom of your large sundae dish.

2. Add ¼ cup mixed fruit.

3. Add all of your granola.

4. Add another ¼ cup mixed fruit.

5. Top with the remaining ½ cup of Milano cookies.

6. Add vanilla ice cream and caramel ice cream.

7. Top with *Purin* and the remaining ½ cup of mixed fruit.

8. Garnish with Apricot Yuzu Marshmallows and a maraschino cherry, as well as other bite-sized cookies or snacks from this book, such as *Chibi Dorayaki*, Pocky (page 34), or *Dango* Dumplings (pages 37–38).

APRICOT YUZU MARSHMALLOWS

Time: 30 minutes plus 3 hours refrigeration • **Yield:** Sixteen 2-inch marshmallow squares

¼ cup powdered sugar

¼ cup cornstarch

Nonstick cooking spray

4 teaspoons powdered gelatin

¼ cup cold water

⅔ cup puréed apricot

2¼ cups sugar

1 teaspoon yuzu extract

½ cup corn syrup

1 large pinch salt

3 large egg whites

1. Line an 8-by-8-inch square baking pan with plastic wrap. In a small bowl, mix the powdered sugar with the cornstarch. Spray the plastic-lined pan with nonstick cooking spray, then liberally dust it with half of the cornstarch and powdered sugar mixture using a fine mesh sieve.

2. In another small bowl, sprinkle the gelatin into cold water and mix to incorporate. Let sit for 5 minutes.

3. In a medium saucepan over medium heat, combine the puréed apricot, sugar, yuzu extract, corn syrup, and salt. Cook until a candy thermometer reads 240°F, about 8 minutes, and then take the pan off the heat.

4. While the apricot mixture is cooking, microwave the gelatin mixture for 10 seconds and stir. Whisk it together with the apricot mixture after the bubbles in the apricot mixture have subsided.

5. In a stand mixer, whisk the egg whites on high speed until soft peaks form. Continue mixing at high speed as you pour the gelatin and apricot mixture into the mixing bowl.

6. Pour the marshmallow mixture into your prepared pan. Smooth the top of the mixture with a small offset spatula and dust it with the remaining cornstarch and powdered sugar mixture. Cover and refrigerate for at least 3 hours.

7. Using a sharp knife, separate the edges of the marshmallow from the sides of the pan. Cover the pan with a cutting board, flip the pan over, and drop the marshmallow onto the cutting board. Cut the marshmallow into 2-inch squares, then place the marshmallow squares in a medium bowl with the remaining sugar and cornstarch mixture and toss the squares until all of their sides are covered.

8. Store in an airtight container at room temperature for up to 1 week.

JAPANESE CHRISTMAS CAKE

Time: 2 hours plus 30 minutes cooling time • **Yield:** One 8-inch cake

Christmas cakes, or *kurisumasu kēki*, are ubiquitous in Japan during the holiday season. This decadent dessert first arrived after World War II, when the Japanese economy was reeling and sugary treats were scarce. American soldiers handing out chocolate and other candies led to sweets becoming an aspirational symbol for prosperity and Americanization, and Christmas began to be celebrated as the epitome of abundance. In anime, Christmas cakes are often enjoyed at parties during a moment of calm and togetherness before a big season finale.

Between each layer of this decadent chiffon cake is fresh whipped cream and juicy strawberries cut into quarters. On top is even more whipped cream and strawberries, and you can also add sugared rosemary or a fresh sprig of mint for a pop of green and some holiday spirit.

CAKE

Nonstick cooking spray

½ cup vegetable oil

6 large eggs, yolks and whites separated

¾ cup whole milk

2½ cups all-purpose flour, sifted

1½ cups granulated sugar, divided

2 teaspoons baking powder

½ teaspoon cream of tartar

2 teaspoons vanilla extract

2 cups strawberries, hulled and quartered

5 fresh whole strawberries, hulled

1 sprig fresh mint or candied rosemary

WHIPPED CREAM

4 cups cold heavy whipping cream

8 tablespoons granulated sugar

4 teaspoons vanilla extract

1. Preheat your oven to 325°F.

TO MAKE THE CAKE:

1. Lightly spray two 8-inch round cake pans with nonstick cooking spray, then line the bottom of each pan with a round cutout of parchment paper.

2. Using a stand mixer or an electric hand mixer and medium bowl, whisk together the oil, egg yolks, and milk. In a separate bowl, mix together the flour, ¾ cup of the sugar, and the baking powder. Add this mixture to the egg mixture and whisk until combined.

3. In a clean bowl, begin to beat the egg whites using either a stand mixer or an electric hand mixer on medium speed, until the egg whites turn slightly opaque. Add the cream of tartar to the egg white mixture and continue to beat. The eggs will start to thicken and change to a white color. Add the remaining ¾ cup sugar and continue beating for another 2 minutes. Then add the vanilla extract and continue to mix the meringue until combined.

4. Fold the meringue mixture into the cake batter using a large wooden spoon or rubber spatula. I recommend doing this in stages, mixing gently so that the meringue doesn't deflate. Mix until ingredients are evenly distributed and there are no clumps.

5. Pour an even amount of the combined batter into each of the lined cake pans. Lightly tap the pans against your countertop to help any large air bubbles escape. Bake on the middle rack for 1 hour, checking from time to time to make sure the cake is not browning too quickly. If the top is browning, lower your heat to roughly 310°F.

6. Check that the cakes are cooked by inserting a toothpick into their centers. If the toothpick doesn't come out clean, continue to bake and monitor. Once the cakes are done, let them cool completely before gently removing them from their pans, about 30 minutes.

7. Torte each cake by cutting it in half horizontally with a bread knife, so that you end up with 4 equal discs. Remove the rounded top of each cake and set aside.

TO MAKE THE WHIPPED CREAM:

1. Add the heavy cream, sugar, and vanilla in a cold stand mixer bowl fitted with a whisk attachment. Beat on medium speed for 4 minutes until soft peaks form. The whipped cream should still have a spreadable consistency.

2. Affix the bottom layer of the cake to a cake board using a dollop of the whipped cream. Using a small offset spatula, spread an even layer of whipped cream on top of the cake. Sprinkle either half or a third of your quartered strawberries onto the whipped cream layer, depending on how many layers you intend to build.

3. Repeat the previous step, adding the remaining pieces of cake on top of the layers of whipped cream and strawberries until the cake is either three or four layers high. (If you stop at three, feel free to snack on that extra piece while decorating!) For added stability, you may want to chill the cake after adding each layer to let the whipped cream firm up in the refrigerator.

4. Using an offset spatula, smooth whipped cream around the sides of the entire cake and apply whipped cream liberally to the top of the cake. You can either make the top smooth like the sides or sculpt the whipped cream to mimic snowdrifts!

5. Decorate the top of the cake with 5 whole fresh strawberries, making sure that they are completely dry. Garnish with a sprig of fresh mint.

AS SEEN IN: *Saint Young Men; Himouto! Umaru-chan; Cheer Boys!!; Log Horizon*

In the slice-of-life comedy *Saint Young Men*, Buddha and Jesus are roommates sharing an apartment in Tokyo. At Christmastime, Jesus forgets that it is his birthday (he has an extreme admiration for Santa Claus and believes that the main significance of Christmas is commemorating the day that Santa achieved reindeer-propelled flight). Buddha takes advantage of his roommate's absentmindedness to throw him a surprise birthday party, where he presents a Christmas cake adorned with a Santa figure to a delighted Jesus. Make your next holiday party extra special as well with this crowd-pleasing confection!

CHRISTMAS CUPCAKES

Time: 1 hour 30 minutes • **Yield:** 12 cupcakes

Make the mini version of a Japanese Christmas cake!

CUPCAKES

¼ cup vegetable oil

3 large eggs, yolks and whites separated

1/3 cup whole milk

1¼ cups all-purpose flour, sifted

1 teaspoon baking powder

¼ teaspoon cream of tartar

¾ cup granulated sugar

1 teaspoon vanilla extract

3 stalks fresh mint

WHIPPED CREAM

2 cups cold heavy whipping cream

4 tablespoons granulated sugar

2 teaspoons vanilla extract

MINI SANTA FIGURES

18 strawberries, hulled

¼ cup mini chocolate chips

1. Preheat your oven to 325°F.

2. Line a cupcake tray with 12 paper cupcake liners.

TO MAKE THE CUPCAKES:

1. In a stand mixer or electric hand mixer and medium bowl, whisk together the oil, egg yolks, and milk. In a separate bowl, mix together the flour and the baking powder. Add this mixture to the egg mixture and whisk until combined.

2. In a clean bowl, begin to beat the egg whites using either a stand mixer or an electric hand mixer on medium speed, until the egg whites turn slightly opaque. Add the cream of tartar to the egg white mixture and continue beating. The eggs will start to thicken and change to a white color. Add the sugar and continue to beat for another 4 minutes on high until soft peaks form. Then add the vanilla extract and continue to mix the meringue until combined.

3. Fold the meringue mixture into the cupcake batter using a large wooden spoon or rubber spatula. I recommend doing this in stages, mixing gently so that the meringue doesn't deflate. Mix until ingredients are evenly distributed and there are no clumps.

4. Pour an even amount of the batter into each of the cupcake liners, ¾ full. Lightly tap the pan against your countertop to help any large air bubbles escape. Bake on the middle rack for 30 minutes.

5. Check that the cupcakes are cooked by inserting a toothpick into their centers. If the toothpick doesn't come out clean, continue to bake and monitor. Once the cupcakes are done, let them cool completely before gently removing them from their pans.

TO MAKE THE WHIPPED CREAM:

1. Add the heavy cream, sugar, and vanilla extract in a cold stand mixer bowl fitted with a whisk attachment. Beat on medium speed for 4 minutes until soft peaks form. The whipped cream should still have a spreadable consistency.

2. Using a small offset spatula, frost each cupcake with whipped cream.

TO MAKE THE MINI SANTA FIGURES:

1. After making sure that the strawberries are dry, cut off the small end of each strawberry and pipe on a quarter-sized dollop of whipped cream. Place the strawberry tip on top of the whipped cream, and add 2 small chocolate chips for eyes.

2. Top each cupcake with a Santa and a sprig of fresh mint.

MATCHA SWISS ROLL CAKE

Time: 2 hours 30 minutes plus 2 hours refrigeration • **Yield:** 1 matcha Swiss roll, cut into 8 pieces

For this recipe, be sure to use a jelly roll sheet pan, which has a 1-inch rim, rather than a typical sheet pan intended for cookies or roasting.

SWISS ROLL

Nonstick cooking spray

1 cup cake flour

2 tablespoons matcha powder

½ teaspoon baking powder

4 large eggs, separated, with whites chilled and yolks at room temperature

½ cup sugar, divided

2 tablespoons whole milk

½ cup *tsubu an* (coarse Red Bean Paste, page 12)

MATCHA WHIPPED CREAM

1½ cups cold heavy whipping cream

3 tablespoons sugar

1 tablespoon matcha powder

AS SEEN IN: *Yumeiro Patissiere; Princess Jellyfish; ACCA: 13-Territory Inspection Dept.*

In *Yumeiro Patissiere*, Sennosuke Andou dreams of combining East and West in a new shop next to his family's traditional *wagashiya*. His little brother Ichita is upset that Sennosuke wants to branch out instead of focusing on the family business, but in episode 4, Sennosuke bakes a matcha roll cake using red bean paste made by Ichita, and the result is an ideal fraternal collaboration. Experience the pairing of Japanese and Western sweets for yourself with this impeccable matcha roll cake!

1. Preheat your oven to 375°F.

TO MAKE THE SWISS ROLL:

1. Line a 15-by-10-inch jelly roll pan with parchment paper and lightly spray with nonstick cooking spray. Prepare two additional parchment paper pieces of the same size and set them aside.

3. In a large bowl, sift the flour and matcha powder and whisk together with the baking powder.

4. In a second large bowl, whisk together the egg yolks. Whisk ¼ cup sugar into the yolks until they take on a ribbon texture.

5. In a third large bowl, whisk the chilled egg whites until they achieve a foamy consistency. Then add the remaining ¼ cup sugar and continue to whisk until stiff peaks form and the meringue has a glossy sheen.

6. Slowly mix ⅓ of the meringue mixture into the egg yolk mixture. Then pour the meringue and egg yolk mixture into the bowl with the remaining meringue and carefully fold the two components together with a rubber spatula, until they are just combined. Do not overmix.

7. Add the flour and matcha mixture to the meringue mixture, continuing to fold them in with the spatula. Then add the milk and fold until incorporated.

8. Pour the batter into the prepared pan and smooth the surface with an offset spatula. Lightly tap the pan against your countertop to help any large air bubbles escape. Bake for 10 minutes on the middle rack, or until a toothpick comes out clean.

9. Remove the cake from the oven and let cool for 1 minute. Place a second piece of parchment paper on top of your cake in the pan while it is still warm. Then, using oven mitts, flip the pan onto a clean work surface. Remove the parchment paper that was on the bottom of the pan and place a new piece of parchment paper on top of the cake. Make sure that the brown side of the cake is facing up.

10. Slowly roll up the warm cake and the parchment paper into a cylinder. (You may want to use a lightweight kitchen towel to avoid burning yourself.) Tuck a lightweight towel over your cake roll and let it cool completely, about 1 hour. The towel should hold your roll in place.

TO MAKE THE MATCHA WHIPPED CREAM:

1. While waiting for the cake roll to cool, beat the heavy whipping cream and sugar together using a stand mixer with a whisk attachment or a hand mixer on high speed. Continue to beat until the mixture is spreadable like frosting, about 5 minutes, but not so soft that it will leak out of the sides of your cake. Add the matcha powder and mix for an additional 10 seconds, or until the matcha is evenly distributed.

2. Once the cake roll is cool, unroll it. Leaving a ½-inch border at the margins, spread the matcha whipped cream over the center of the brown interior side of your cake.

3. Add the *tsubu an* to the edge of the cake where you will start to roll it up toward the cake's middle.

4. Slowly reroll the cake, taking care that the filling doesn't ooze out. Wrap your cake roll in parchment paper or plastic wrap so that it holds its shape, and refrigerate for 2 hours with the seam of the cake's covering facing down.

5. Before serving, slice off one end of the cake with a sharp bread knife to expose the interior swirl (and enjoy it as a reward for a job well done!).

6. Slice to your desired width (I recommend dividing into 8 pieces) and serve.

BLACK SUGAR SOY SWISS ROLL CAKE

Time: 2 hours 30 minutes plus 2 hours refrigeration • **Yield:** 1 Swiss roll, cut into 8 pieces

AS SEEN IN: *Food Wars!: Shokugeki no Sōma; My Love Story!!; Log Horizon*

In a match against Erina Nakiri in *Food Wars!: Shokugeki no Sōma*, Momo Akanegakubo impresses with her *kawaii* roll cake made with whipped cream that contains a hint of soy sauce. The soy flavor heightens the taste of the brown sugar ingredients, similar to the irresistible combination of sweet and salty notes in salted caramel. You may wish to fill your cake with soy buttercream instead, which is a more stable filling for roll cake beginners. Soy sauce whipped cream and buttercream are truly a delicacy—whip up this umami dessert, and you will be more than a match for any challenger!

Black sugar is a specialty product of Okinawa. You can use dark brown sugar or dark muscovado sugar for this recipe if black sugar is not easily sourced in your area.

SWISS ROLL

Nonstick cooking spray

1¼ cups all-purpose flour

1 teaspoon baking powder

½ teaspoon baking soda

1 large pinch salt

4 large eggs, at room temperature

1 cup *kurozato* (Okinawan black sugar), dark muscovado sugar, or dark brown sugar, divided

½ cup buttermilk

⅓ cup vegetable or canola oil

1 teaspoon vanilla extract

SOY WHIPPED CREAM

1½ cups heavy whipping cream

3 tablespoons sugar

1 teaspoon soy sauce

OPTIONAL: SOY BUTTERCREAM

1 cup unsalted butter

4 cups powdered sugar

¼ cup heavy whipping cream

1 large pinch salt

2 teaspoons soy sauce

1. Preheat your oven to 375°F.

TO MAKE THE SWISS ROLL:

1. Line a 15-by-10-inch jelly roll pan with parchment paper. Lightly spray with nonstick cooking spray. Prepare two additional parchment paper pieces of the same size and set them aside.

3. In a large bowl, sift the flour and whisk it together with the baking powder, baking soda, and salt.

4. In a separate large bowl, whisk together the room temperature eggs with ¾ cup of the *kurozato* or dark muscovado sugar. Whisk the buttermilk, oil, and vanilla extract into the egg mixture until combined, then whisk the dry ingredients into the wet mixture.

5. Pour the batter into the prepared pan and smooth the surface with an offset spatula. Lightly tap the pan against your countertop to help any large air bubbles escape. Bake for 20 minutes on the middle rack, or until a toothpick comes out clean.

6. Remove the cake from the oven and let cool for 1 minute. Place a second piece of parchment paper on top of your cake in the pan while it is still warm. Then, using oven mitts, flip the pan onto your clean work surface. Remove the parchment paper that was on the bottom of the pan and place a new piece of parchment paper on top of the cake. Make sure that the brown side of the cake is facing up.

7. Slowly roll up the warm cake and the parchment paper into a cylinder. (You may want to use a lightweight kitchen towel to avoid burning yourself.) Tuck a lightweight towel over your cake roll and let it cool completely, about 1 hour. The towel should hold your roll in place.

TO MAKE THE SOY WHIPPED CREAM:

1. While waiting for the cake to cool, beat the heavy whipping cream and sugar together using a stand mixer with a whisk attachment or a hand mixer on high speed. Continue to beat until the mixture is spreadable like frosting, about 5 minutes, but not so soft that it will leak out of the sides of your cake. Add the soy sauce and mix for an additional 10 seconds.

TO MAKE THE SOY BUTTERCREAM:

1. While waiting for the cake to cool, beat the butter and sugar together in a stand mixer with a paddle attachment on high speed. Add powdered sugar in two stages, then add heavy whipping cream and salt. Add 2 teaspoons soy sauce, or to taste, and beat until combined.

2. Once the cake roll is cool, unroll it. Leaving a ½-inch border at the margins, spread the soy whipped cream or buttercream over the brown interior side of your cake and sprinkle on the remaining ¼ cup of the *kurozato*.

3. Slowly reroll the cake, taking care that the filling doesn't ooze out. Wrap the cake roll in parchment paper or plastic wrap so that it holds its shape, and refrigerate for 2 hours with the seam of the cake's covering facing down.

4. Before serving, slice off one end of your cake with a sharp bread knife to expose the interior swirl (and enjoy the results of your hard work!).

5. Slice to your desired width (I recommend dividing into 8 pieces) and serve.

VALENTINE'S DAY CHOCOLATE CAKE

Time: 2 hours • **Yield:** 8 thick slices of loaf cake

AS SEEN IN: *K-On!!; Log Horizon; Yumeiro Patissiere*

For Valentine's Day, Azusa Nakano decides to make a chocolate cake to give to her senpais in the Light Music Club during episode 22 of *K-On!!*. When the day comes, however, she can't seem to work up the courage to present the cake. Though her other friends think she is being shy, Azusa is also sad that her senpais are graduating soon and their time together is drawing to a close. Fortunately, she overcomes her anxiety and is able to share the cake, which is universally praised.

Celebrate Valentine's Day and the impermanence of all things with this decadent two-layer cake, just like the one Azusa whips up!

CAKE

Nonstick cooking spray

2 cups sugar

1 cup canola oil

½ cup sour cream

2 extra-large eggs

2½ cups all-purpose flour

1 cup cocoa powder

2½ teaspoons baking powder

½ teaspoon baking soda

1 large pinch salt

1 cup brewed coffee

BUTTERCREAM

1 cup unsalted butter, at room temperature

4 cups powdered sugar

½ cup cocoa powder

5 tablespoons heavy whipping cream

1 pinch salt

½ teaspoon vanilla extract

CHOCOLATE GLAZE

2 tablespoons unsalted butter

1/3 cup chopped high quality milk chocolate or milk chocolate chips

1 cup powdered sugar

2 tablespoons boiling water

TO MAKE THE CAKE:

1. Line a 9-by-5-by-2½-inch loaf pan with parchment paper and spray with nonstick cooking spray.

2. Preheat your oven to 350°F.

3. In a stand mixer, mix the sugar and oil together on medium speed. Add the sour cream and the eggs, and mix to combine.

4. In a separate large mixing bowl, mix together the flour, cocoa powder, baking powder, baking soda, and salt. Add the dry ingredients to the wet ingredients in three stages, mixing on low speed until combined. Then add the brewed coffee and mix until incorporated.

5. Pour the batter into your prepared loaf pan and bake on the middle rack for 50 minutes, or until an inserted toothpick comes out clean.

TO MAKE THE BUTTERCREAM:

1. While the cake is baking, beat the butter in a stand mixer on medium speed with a paddle attachment until it is light and fluffy. Turn the speed to low and add the powdered sugar, 1 cup at a time. Add the cocoa powder, heavy whipping cream, salt, and vanilla extract, and beat to combine. Set aside.

TO MAKE THE CHOCOLATE GLAZE:

1. Combine the butter and the chopped milk chocolate in a medium saucepan over low heat until the chocolate has melted, then remove from heat. Slowly sift your powdered sugar directly into the melted chocolate while constantly whisking. Then add the boiling water to thin out the mixture until it has a fluid, pourable consistency. Set aside.

2. After you've taken the cake out of the oven, let it cool for 15 minutes before removing it from the pan. Once it is completely cool, torte the cake by cutting it in half horizontally with a bread knife and slice off the rounded top of the cake so that you have two flat, evenly sized pieces.

3. Line a sheet pan with plastic wrap and place one piece of cake on it. Using an offset spatula, apply a thick layer of buttercream to the top of the cake. Place the other half of the cake on top of the first. Pour the chocolate glaze over the cake, spreading it across the entire surface and letting it drip down the sides.

4. Chill the cake for 30 minutes in the refrigerator, then cut it into 8 equal pieces with a bread knife to serve.

STRAWBERRY CHOCOLATE CHECKERBOARD ICEBOX COOKIES

Time: 1 hour 50 minutes • **Yield:** 12 checkerboard cookies

These striking cookies are a favorite in anime, likely because of their easily recognizable pattern. Bake a batch to share with someone you have big feelings for!

AS SEEN IN: *Toradora!; Boarding School Juliet; One Week Friends*

In *Toradora!*, the petite but mighty Taiga Aisaka makes checkerboard icebox cookies in a school cooking class to give to her crush, Kitamura. The cookies are a success, but her attempt at presenting them to Kitamura goes dramatically awry.

1 cup unsalted butter, at room temperature

½ cup sugar

1 teaspoon vanilla extract

2 large eggs

2½ cups all-purpose flour

1 large pinch salt

3 tablespoons cocoa powder

2 drops pink gel food coloring

3 teaspoons strawberry extract

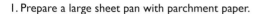

1. Prepare a large sheet pan with parchment paper.

2. In a stand mixer with a paddle attachment, cream together the butter and the sugar on medium speed until light and fluffy, about 1 minute. Add the vanilla extract and 1 egg, and mix to combine.

3. Sift the flour and the salt together. Add the flour mixture to the wet mixture in two stages and mix to combine.

4. Divide the dough into two equal parts. (You may want to weigh the dough with a kitchen scale to be accurate.) In a stand mixer, mix cocoa powder into half of the dough with a paddle attachment on medium speed for about 1 minute, then set the dough aside.

5. Add the food coloring and strawberry extract to the other half of the dough and mix on medium speed to combine in your stand mixer, about 1 minute.

6. Place each piece of dough between two pieces of parchment paper and roll out to 7-by-7-inch squares, about ½ inch thick. Refrigerate the dough for 30 minutes.

7. Using a ruler and a sharp knife or pizza cutter, cut the dough into nine strips, each ¾ inch wide. Cover your work surface with plastic wrap and place three strips of dough side by side, alternating the colors, with their edges touching. Gently push the strips together.

8. Whisk the remaining egg in a small bowl. Using a pastry brush, apply a thin layer of egg wash to the tops of the dough strips.

9. Place three more strips of dough, also alternating the colors, on top of the first set with the strips running perpendicular to those of the first layer. Repeat the process until you run out of dough, or until the cookie log is as wide as you would like it to be.

10. Preheat your oven to 350°F.

11. Wrap the log of cookie dough in plastic wrap and freeze it for 15 minutes, or refrigerate until it's firm, about 40 minutes. Then slice the log into ¼-inch-wide pieces with a sharp knife.

12. Place the cookie pieces on the prepared sheet pan. Bake for 11 minutes on the middle rack.

VALENTINE'S DAY CHOCOLATES

Time: 20 minutes plus 30 minutes refrigeration • **Yield:** 18 chocolates

Valentine's Day in Japan is typically marked by women giving chocolates to men. (Men return the favor on White Day, which falls on March 14.) Chocolate-giving on Valentine's Day can be broken down into three categories: Honmei Choco is chocolate intended for your romantic partner and tends to be more expensive and ornate, or requires more effort if you're making it at home; Tomo Choco is chocolate for your female friends, which is often given out at school (the word *tomo* comes from *tomodachi*, the Japanese word for "friend"); Giri Choco, or "obligation chocolates," are chocolates that you give to your coworkers, family members, and other acquaintances who don't quite fall into the first two categories.

The following variations on Valentine's Day chocolates are sure to delight anyone who receives them. I recommend using high quality bar chocolate or couverture instead of chocolate chips for these recipes. Chocolate chips are made with soybean lecithin to help them hold their shape while baking, and this compound hinders the tempering process. Instead, look for brands like Guittard or Valrhona that contain a high percentage of cocoa butter.

1 cup high quality dark chocolate, chopped

1½ cups high quality white chocolate, chopped

1 teaspoon matcha powder

1 cup Callebaut Ruby Chocolate Callets

1 cup crushed brownie

1 tablespoon assorted sprinkles

AS SEEN IN: *Hinako Note; The Disappearance of Nagato Yuki-chan; Monthly Girls' Nozaki-kun*

In episode 12 of *Hinako Note*, Hinako stumbles into the kitchen late one night and discovers Mayuki stirring a mysterious pot on the stove. Cloaked in a hood, Mayuki is chanting "Aki-chan," Chiyaki's nickname. Hinako immediately fears the worst and wonders if Mayuki is trying to poison Chiyaki. It turns out that she is merely making Valentine's Day chocolates for Chiyaki and has heard that if you chant the name of the person you're making the chocolates for during the process, the special treats will taste better. For optimal results, don't forget to do the same when you make your Valentine's Day chocolates!

1. Place the dark chocolate in a small heatproof bowl and microwave it on medium power for 30 seconds, followed by 20-second, 15-second, and 10-second increments, until the chocolate reaches 115°F on a candy thermometer.

2. Stir the melted chocolate until it cools to between 88° and 90°F. This process of warming and cooling the chocolate is called *tempering*, as seen in the recipe for Pocky Sticks (page 34). After tempering, you can test your chocolate by dabbing a bit of it on a piece of parchment paper. Successfully tempered chocolate will harden and display a shine at room temperature. If your chocolate doesn't do these things, continue to mix the chocolate until it reaches a cooler temperature, or heat it in the microwave in 10-second increments until it reaches the correct temperature.

3. Using a 12-piece silicone mold with heart shapes, paint a thin layer of dark chocolate into 9 of the heart shapes with a small food-safe paintbrush.

4. Using the same process as the dark chocolate, microwave the white chocolate until it reaches 110°F on a candy thermometer. Stir the melted chocolate until the temperature reads 84°F, then stir in the matcha powder. Using a piping bag with a small round tip, pipe the matcha white chocolate into the molds, filling each mold ¾ of the way up the sides. Fill the rest of each mold with the remaining dark chocolate and let set for 10 minutes.

5. Using the same method as for the dark and white chocolate, microwave the ruby chocolate in a small heatproof bowl until the chocolate reaches 110°F on a candy thermometer. Stir the melted chocolate until the temperature reads between 83° and 85°F.

6. Using a separate mold, paint ruby chocolate onto the insides of an additional 9 heart shapes.

7. Pack 2 teaspoons of crushed brownie into each mold with your hands, then cover the crushed brownie with the remaining ruby chocolate. Let set for 10 minutes.

8. Once the chocolate hearts have hardened, carefully remove them from their molds.

9. Prepare a large sheet pan with wax paper and place the dark chocolate hearts on the pan. Then reheat the remaining matcha chocolate and drizzle it over the dark chocolate hearts. Add assorted sprinkles while the chocolate is still wet.

10. Let the chocolates dry for an additional 20 minutes before packing or consuming. Store in an airtight container.

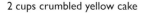

VALENTINE'S DAY
CHOCOLATE HEART

Time: 1 hour plus 50 minutes refrigeration • **Yield:** One 7-inch chocolate heart

2 cups crumbled yellow cake

½ cup buttercream or store-bought frosting

1½ cups high quality white chocolate, chopped

2 drops pink oil-based food coloring

2 drops purple oil-based food coloring

Edible pink luster dust for garnishing

Edible red glitter for garnishing

1. Prepare a small sheet pan by lining it with wax paper.
2. In a medium bowl, mix the crumbled cake and the buttercream (or frosting) to combine.
3. Place the white chocolate in a small heatproof bowl and microwave it on medium power for 30 seconds, followed by 20-second, 15-second, and 10-second increments, until the chocolate reaches 110°F on a candy thermometer.
4. Stir the white chocolate until it cools to between 82° and 84°F, then mix the pink and purple food coloring into the chocolate and swirl to create a marbled effect.
5. Pour half of the chocolate mixture into a large heart-shaped mold and tilt it back and forth to distribute the chocolate evenly. Use a food-safe paintbrush to apply chocolate to any parts of the mold that it didn't reach.
6. Let the chocolate in the mold set for 10 minutes, then use the paintbrush to apply another layer of chocolate to the inside walls of the mold in the same manner. Let this set for an additional 10 minutes.
7. Using a large spoon, pack the cake and frosting mixture into the mold, leaving a little space at the top. Then reheat the white chocolate mixture and pour it into the mold, filling it to the top. Let this set for 20 minutes.
8. Carefully remove the chocolate heart from its mold and place it on the pan.
9. Apply the pink luster dust to the heart's surface with a soft food-safe paintbrush and sprinkle with edible glitter.

NAMA CHOCOLATE

Time: 3 hours 20 minutes • **Yield:** 25 chocolates

Nama chocolate is a silky ganache-style chocolate introduced to Japan in 1988 by chef and pastry shop owner Masakazu Kobayashi. He chose the name as an allusion to the abundance of fresh heavy cream in the recipe, as *nama* means "raw" in Japanese. This chocolate must be kept refrigerated.

1 cup high quality dark chocolate, chopped

¾ cup heavy whipping cream

1 tablespoon unsalted butter

¼ cup matcha powder

1. Line a 5-by-5-inch baking pan with parchment paper and place the chocolate in a medium heatproof bowl.
2. In a medium saucepan, warm the heavy cream and butter over medium heat until it reaches 176°F on a candy thermometer.
3. Pour the cream mixture over the chocolate and whisk until the chocolate is incorporated and has a smooth texture.
4. Pour the chocolate mix into the prepared pan and place it in the freezer for 3 hours.
5. Remove the chocolate from the freezer and use a ruler and a knife to mark 4 evenly spaced cuts, both crosswise and lengthwise, on its surface. Following the marked measurements, cut the chocolate into squares with a warm knife. Then dust matcha powder onto the chocolate squares using a fine mesh sieve.
6. To store, refrigerate in an airtight container.

RARE CHEESECAKE

Time: 3 hours 30 minutes • **Yield:** One 7-inch cheesecake

Rare cheesecake is a Japanese variety of the dessert that gets its firmness from refrigeration rather than heat. Its original flavor, which combines classic cheesecake flavor with a hint of lemon, pairs well with fresh fruit, fruit sauces, and fresh mint. These recipes call for gelatin, but you can also use kanten to achieve the same consistency. And remember: *Always* chill your cheesecakes for at least 3 hours before cutting and serving!

CHEESECAKE

Nonstick cooking spray

1 tablespoon gelatin powder

¼ cup cold water

1½ cups cream cheese, softened

¾ cup plain Greek yogurt

⅔ cup sugar

2 tablespoons lemon juice

CRUST

2 cups graham crackers, crushed into fine pieces

6 tablespoons unsalted butter, melted

2 tablespoons packed light brown sugar

1 pinch salt

RASPBERRY SAUCE

1 cup sugar

⅓ cup plus 2 tablespoons water

2 cups frozen raspberries

2 tablespoons cornstarch

1 teaspoon lemon juice

1 teaspoon vanilla extract

Salt

TO MAKE THE CHEESECAKE:

1. Spray a 7-inch springform pan with nonstick cooking spray.

2. In a small heatproof bowl, mix the gelatin powder with cold water. Let sit for 5 minutes.

3. In a stand mixer with a paddle attachment, beat the cream cheese, yogurt, sugar, and lemon juice together on medium speed.

4. Microwave the gelatin mixture on medium power for 10 seconds, then add it to the cake batter and beat on medium speed until combined, about 10 seconds.

TO MAKE THE CRUST:

1. In a separate bowl, combine the graham cracker crumbs, butter, sugar, and salt. Pack the bottom of the springform pan with an even layer of the resulting mix.

2. Pour the cake batter into the pan on top of the graham cracker crust. Refrigerate for 3 hours, or until the cake has set.

TO MAKE THE RASPBERRY SAUCE:

1. While the cheesecake is chilling, heat a small saucepan over medium heat and add the sugar, ⅓ cup water, and the frozen raspberries. Stir continuously as the sugar dissolves, and cook until the mixture comes to a boil. Remove from heat.

2. In a small bowl, mix the cornstarch with the remaining 2 tablespoons of water and the lemon juice. Add the cornstarch mixture and the vanilla extract to the raspberry mixture and stir until combined. Finish the raspberry sauce with a sprinkle of salt, then chill the mixture so that it doesn't melt the cheesecake when they come into contact.

3. Serve each slice of cheesecake with a heaping spoonful of raspberry sauce.

AS SEEN IN: *Cardcaptor Sakura: Clear Card; High School Fleet; Brynhildr in the Darkness*

In episode 2 of *Cardcaptor Sakura: Clear Card*, Chiharu gives Sakura and Tomoyo her rare cheesecake recipe. Sakura and Tomoyo make the recipe with the help of Kero-chan, Sakura's furry winged guardian. The rare cheesecake with raspberry sauce hits the spot, and Sakura realizes that even though she has a lot on her mind, spending time worrying won't help, and she resolves to continue to do her best. Allow your worries to melt away as well as you prepare this luxurious confection!

RARE BLACK SESAME CHEESECAKE

Time: 3 hours 30 minutes • **Yield:** One 7-inch cheesecake

CHEESECAKE

Nonstick cooking spray

1 tablespoon gelatin powder

¼ cup cold water

1½ cups cream cheese, softened

¾ cup plain Greek yogurt

⅔ cup sugar

½ tablespoon lemon juice

¼ cup black sesame paste

CRUST

2 cups chocolate shortbread cookies, crushed into fine pieces

6 tablespoons unsalted butter, melted

2 tablespoons packed dark brown sugar

6 tablespoons black sesame seeds

1 pinch salt

BLACK SESAME TUILE

¾ cup black sesame seeds

1¼ cups sugar

½ cup all-purpose flour

4 tablespoons unsalted butter, melted

½ tablespoon black sesame paste

½ cup orange juice

¼ cup black and white sesame seeds for garnishing

TO MAKE THE CHEESECAKE:

1. Spray a 7-inch springform pan with nonstick cooking spray.

2. In a small heatproof bowl, mix the gelatin powder with cold water. Let sit for 5 minutes.

3. In a stand mixer with a paddle attachment, beat the cream cheese, yogurt, sugar, and lemon juice together on medium speed.

4. Microwave the gelatin mixture on medium power for 10 seconds, then add it to the cake batter and beat on medium speed until combined, about 10 seconds. Mix in black sesame paste and continue beating on medium speed until the batter is uniformly colored.

TO MAKE THE CRUST:

1. In a separate bowl, combine the chocolate shortbread cookie crumbs, butter, sugar, black sesame seeds, and salt. Pack the bottom of the springform pan with an even layer of the chocolate shortbread cookie mix.

2. Pour the cake batter into the pan on top of the cookie crust. Refrigerate for 3 hours, or until the cake has set.

3. Preheat your oven to 350°F.

TO MAKE THE BLACK SESAME TUILE:

1. While the cheesecake is chilling, pulse ¾ cup of black sesame seeds in a spice grinder. In a medium bowl, whisk the ground sesame seeds together with the sugar and the flour.

2. In a separate bowl, mix the melted butter and the black sesame paste.

3. Stir the orange juice into the flour mixture, then whisk the butter and black sesame paste mixture into the same bowl. Let rest for 1 hour at room temperature.

4. Spread the tuile batter on a large sheet pan lined with parchment paper, forming a very thin layer with an offset spatula. Sprinkle the top of the batter with ¼ cup mix of black and white sesame seeds.

5. Bake for 3 minutes on the middle rack of your oven.

6. Once the cheesecake has been refrigerated for 3 hours, crackle the black sesame tuile on top to garnish.

RARE YAKULT CHEESECAKE WITH LEMON CURD

Time: 3 hours 30 minutes • **Yield:** One 9-inch cheesecake

Yakult is a popular probiotic milk beverage that is a staple of Japanese supermarkets and convenience stores. The tangy drink comes in small 2.7-ounce bottles, which are often sold in multipacks.

CHEESECAKE

Nonstick cooking spray

2 tablespoons gelatin powder

½ cup cold water

3 cups cream cheese, softened

1 cup plain Greek yogurt

1⅓ cup sugar

Four 2.7-ounce containers Yakult

2 tablespoons lemon juice

CRUST

4 cups gingersnap cookies, crushed into fine pieces

12 tablespoons unsalted butter, melted

4 tablespoons sugar

1 pinch salt

LEMON CURD

2 large egg yolks

1½ lemons, juiced

1 lemon, zested

⅓ cup sugar

3 tablespoons unsalted butter, at room temperature

TO MAKE THE CHEESECAKE:

1. Spray an 9-inch springform pan with nonstick cooking spray.

2. In a small heatproof bowl, mix the gelatin powder with cold water. Let sit for 5 minutes.

3. In a stand mixer with a paddle attachment, beat the cream cheese, yogurt, sugar, Yakult, and lemon juice together on medium speed.

4. Microwave the gelatin mixture on medium power for 10 seconds, then add it to the cake batter and beat on medium speed until combined, about 10 seconds.

TO MAKE THE CRUST:

1. In a separate bowl, combine the gingersnap cookie crumbs, butter, sugar, and salt. Pack the bottom of the springform pan with an even layer of the gingersnap cookie mix.

2. Pour cake batter into the pan on top of the gingersnap crust. Refrigerate for 3 hours, or until the cake has set.

TO MAKE THE LEMON CURD:

1. While the cheesecake is chilling, make a double boiler by filling a medium pan with 1 inch of water and placing another pan on top of it, so that the bottom of the top pan does not touch the water below. Bring the water to a boil and then lower the heat to medium.

3. Whisk together the egg yolks, lemon juice, lemon zest, and sugar in the top of the double boiler. Continue whisking for 10 minutes, making sure that the eggs don't scramble. The mix should integrate and have a sauce-like consistency.

4. Take the egg mixture off the heat and mix in the butter until it is incorporated. Strain the mixture through a fine mesh sieve to remove any small cooked egg particles that may have formed.

5. Refrigerate the lemon curd before serving. Use as a garnish on the Yakult cheesecake.

HARAJUKU-STYLE CRÊPES

Stuffed crêpes are a popular item in Harajuku, where stands and shops sell many variations of the dish. Crêpes are thin, French-style pancakes that have evolved into a delicious new form in Japan that is especially popular with young people. This recipe for Tutti Frutti Crêpes resembles the crêpe that Kyouka ordered. The Nutella Cream Crêpes (page 121) are another popular flavor.

AS SEEN IN: *Bungo Stray Dogs; Magic-kyun! Renaissance; Is It Wrong to Try to Pick Up Girls in a Dungeon?*

In episode 9 of *Bungo Stray Dogs*, private detective Atsushi Nakajima meets Kyouka, a female assassin who has been forced into the profession by the mafia. Sympathizing with her plight, Atsushi shows her around Yokohama before taking her to the police, and they happen upon a popular crêpe stand. Kyouka orders a decadent stuffed crêpe with pink ice cream, strawberries, blueberries, fresh mint, whipped cream, and a straw-shaped wafer cookie. Why not live for the moment yourself, and indulge in some Harajuku-style crêpes today?

TUTTI FRUTTI CRÊPES

Time: 1 hour • **Yield:** 2 stuffed crêpes

5 tablespoons unsalted butter

1 cup all-purpose flour

½ cup plus 1 tablespoon sugar

1 large pinch salt

1 cup water

2 large eggs

1 teaspoon vanilla extract

¼ cup sliced fresh strawberries

¼ cup fresh blueberries

4 large scoops black cherry or bubblegum ice cream

2 straw wafer cookies

½ cup whipped cream

Fresh mint for garnishing

1. Separate 3 tablespoons of butter into a small heatproof bowl. Microwave the butter on medium power for 30 seconds, or until the butter has liquefied.

2. In a large bowl, combine the melted butter with the flour, 1 tablespoon sugar, salt, water, eggs, and vanilla extract. Mix until smooth, then cover the batter with plastic wrap and refrigerate for 30 minutes.

3. In a medium bowl, mix the strawberries and blueberries together and add the remaining ½ cup sugar.

4. Cut two pieces of parchment paper into triangle shapes, then roll them into paper cones. Tuck in the extra paper to hold the cone in place.

5. Remove the batter from the refrigerator.

6. Heat a medium saucepan over medium-high heat. Grease with 1 tablespoon of your remaining 4 tablespoons of butter, tilting the pan as it heats to make sure the butter covers every inch of it.

7. Pour ½ cup of batter onto the pan and twirl it so that the batter extends to the pan's full width. Cook for 1 minute, then flip the crêpe with a large fish spatula and cook the other side for 1 additional minute. Remove from heat.

8. Add more butter to the pan and repeat the process with the remaining batter.

9. Place 2 large scoops of macerated berries on each crêpe, then fold the crêpes in half while they are still warm.

10. Add 1 scoop of ice cream and a straw wafer cookie to the rounded side of each crêpe. Then roll the crêpes into cone shapes so that the top of the wafer cookie is visible at the open end.

11. Place your rolled crêpes in the parchment paper cones and add an additional scoop of ice cream to each crêpe.

12. Pipe the whipped cream over the ice cream and garnish with fresh mint.

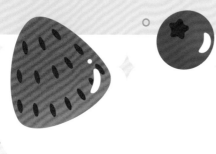

NUTELLA CREAM CRÊPES

Time: 1 hour • **Yield:** 2 stuffed crêpes

5 tablespoons butter

1 cup all-purpose flour

1 tablespoon sugar

1 large pinch salt

1 cup water

2 large eggs

1 teaspoon vanilla extract

4 tablespoons chocolate hazelnut
spread (such as Nutella)

½ cup whipped cream

¼ cup chopped hazelnuts

1 teaspoon cocoa powder

1. Separate 3 tablespoons of butter into a small heatproof bowl. Microwave the butter on medium power for 30 seconds, or until the butter has liquefied.

2. In a large bowl, combine the melted butter with the flour, sugar, salt, water, eggs, and vanilla extract. Mix until smooth, then cover the batter with plastic wrap and refrigerate for 30 minutes.

3. Cut two pieces of parchment paper into triangle shapes, then roll them into paper cones. Tuck in the extra paper to hold the cone in place.

4. Remove the batter from the refrigerator.

5. Heat a medium saucepan over medium-high heat. Grease with 1 tablespoon of your remaining 4 tablespoons of butter, tilting the pan as it heats to make sure the butter covers every inch of it.

6. Pour ½ cup of batter onto the pan and twirl it so that the batter extends to the pan's full width. Cook for 1 minute, then flip the crêpe with a large fish spatula and cook the other side for 1 additional minute. Remove from heat.

7. Add more butter to the pan and repeat the process with the remaining batter.

8. Spread 2 tablespoons of Nutella on each crêpe while they are still warm, maintaining a 1-inch margin around the edge. Fold the crêpes in half, then roll them into cones.

9. Place your rolled crêpes in the parchment paper cones and pipe the whipped cream into the open end of each crêpe. Garnish with chopped hazelnuts and dust with cocoa powder using a fine mesh sieve.

MELON SODA FLOAT

Time: 20 minutes • **Yield:** 2 medium (6-ounce) soda floats

Melon soda floats are a popular café treat in Japan, and bottles of melon soda are often sold from vending machines and in convenience stores. Melon soda floats first gained popularity in the 1970s, and while café culture has changed since then, the drink is still a pervasive refreshment in Japan.

½ medium fresh honeydew melon, peeled, seeded, cubed, and chilled

4 tablespoons simple syrup

2 drops bright green food coloring (optional)

½ cup soda water, chilled

2 scoops vanilla ice cream

2 maraschino cherries

1. Pulse the fresh honeydew melon cubes with the simple syrup in a blender until the mixture is thick and pulpy. Add bright green food coloring and pulse until the color is evenly distributed.

2. Add the chilled soda water and mix with a spoon until incorporated.

3. Remove the melon mixture from the blender and divide it into two large sundae glasses.

4. Add 1 scoop of vanilla ice cream to each glass, and top each with a maraschino cherry.

AS SEEN IN: *Hetalia: Axis Powers; Restaurant to Another World; Working!!*

The characters in *Hetalia: Axis Powers* are personifications of the world's countries, including a child who represents the tiny micronation of Sealand. Sealand's dream is to be recognized as a real country, a goal he works toward by attending a world conference meeting in episode 21. After getting the cold shoulder from the bigger, more established nations, Sealand is seen sitting at a table taking comfort in his favorite drink: a melon soda float. In anime, melon soda floats are typically consumed by children or childish characters, and drinking one probably doesn't help Sealand in his quest to be taken seriously. But maybe it's okay to be a kid once in a while with a drink this delicious!

MEASUREMENT CONVERSION CHARTS

VOLUME

U.S.	METRIC
⅕ teaspoon (tsp)	1 ml
1 teaspoon (tsp)	5 ml
1 tablespoon (tbsp)	15 ml
1 fluid ounce (fl. oz.)	30 ml
⅕ cup	50 ml
¼ cup	60 ml
⅓ cup	80 ml
3.4 fluid ounces (fl. oz.)	100 ml
½ cup	120 ml
⅔ cup	160 ml
¾ cup	180 ml
1 cup	240 ml
1 pint (2 cups)	480 ml
1 quart (4 cups)	.95 liter

WEIGHT

U.S.	METRIC
0.5 ounce (oz.)	14 grams
1 ounce (oz.)	28 grams
¼ pound (lbs.)	113 grams
⅓ pound (lbs.)	151 grams
½ pound (lbs.)	227 grams
1 pound (lbs.)	454 grams

TEMPERATURES

FAHRENHEIT	CELSIUS
200°	93.3°
212°	100°
250°	120°
275°	135°
300°	150°
325°	165°
350°	177°
400°	205°
425°	220°
450°	233°
475°	245°
500°	260°

ANIME INDEX

ABOUT THE AUTHOR

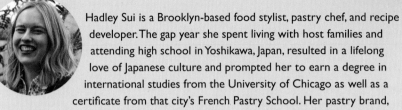

Hadley Sui is a Brooklyn-based food stylist, pastry chef, and recipe developer. The gap year she spent living with host families and attending high school in Yoshikawa, Japan, resulted in a lifelong love of Japanese culture and prompted her to earn a degree in international studies from the University of Chicago as well as a certificate from that city's French Pastry School. Her pastry brand, Hadley Go Lucky, has been featured in pop-ups throughout New York City, and she has also appeared as a guest chef for the Japan Arts Foundation's Tokyo House Party program. *Oishisou!! The Ultimate Anime Dessert Cookbook* represents the culmination of Hadley's favorite pastry recipes inspired by both anime and her experiences in Japan. When outside the kitchen, Hadley can be found going on hikes with her husband, Jackson, and pet, Shiba Yatsuhashi (named after one of Kyoto's specialty pastries); getting lost in a book; and hunting for treasures at the Union Square Greenmarket. Learn more about Hadley at www.hadleysui.com.

ABOUT THE ILLUSTRATOR

Monique "Mo" Narboneta Zosa is an LA-based graphic designer and (more recently) illustrator by trade. From selling fan art at anime conventions in 2012 to publishing her first printed "doodles" in DC Comics' *Harley's Little Black Book* in 2017, illustration has been an enduring aspect of her design career. In 2021, Mo helped to elevate the voice of Sakura Kasugano in Insight Editions' *Street Fighter: The Official Street Food Cookbook* by sprinkling her emoji-style illustrations and other drawings throughout the book. *Oishisou!! The Ultimate Anime Dessert Cookbook* marks Mo's official debut as an illustrator, giving her the opportunity to combine her love of anime, design, and illustration into one delicious publication. Fun fact: Mo's favorite anime of all time is *Tiger and Bunny*! Check out more of her work at monarboneta.com.

ACKNOWLEDGMENTS

I couldn't have written this book without the love and support of my husband and best friend, Jackson. Thanks for watching lots of anime with me! Who would have predicted that I'd be writing about the food in anime when we first started watching *Shokugeki* during our first months together?

Thank you to my family for their support and excitement, and especially to my mom, Jennifer, for facilitating a childhood full of opportunities for creativity and inspiration, and my brother, Brooks. I also want to thank my chosen family of close friends, who helped to cheer me on during the writing process. Many thanks to Chinatsu for her time and insight!

I am forever grateful to the Urbana, Illinois, and Yoshikawa, Saitama, Rotary Clubs for facilitating my high school study abroad experience in Japan in 2010 and 2011. My caring host families, especially Yasuo and Sanae Suzuki, sparked my love for Japan and my constant longing to be back there, where I feel most inspired. I am also grateful to the staff and students at Koshigaya Minami High School, who welcomed me as a member of their community, especially Ueyama Sensei and the members of the cheerleading club.

To my fellow high school exchange students—Jessie, Leona, and Paola—who navigated the amazing experience alongside me, our shared memories bring me so much joy.

Thank you to the professors at the Kyoto Consortium for Japanese Studies at Doshisha University, and to my friends there who were also passionate about the study of Japan and its history, especially Anna and Aubrey. My very first experience writing about *wagashi* was during our Kyoto Artisans class!

Thank you to Hiroko Ito for her time at Uni High. Without your class, I wouldn't have the *Ponyo* theme song committed to memory!

Thank you to my friends at the Japan Arts Foundation, the Consulate-General of Japan at Chicago, the Japan America Society of Chicago, and the Tenri Cultural Institute for allowing me to collaborate and learn from you.

I am also indebted to all the mentors and friends who I have found on my pastry journey. Thank you so much.

Many thanks to Emily Hawkes for photographing this book and to Andrea Greco for incorporating the most whimsical props. I am also so thankful for my food styling assistants, Debbie Wee and Sarah Pleitez, and for photography assistant Regina Tamburro.
I greatly appreciate your help and energy.

I couldn't have written this book without the advice of Alex Shytsman, who was kind enough to share her cookbook experience and encouraged me to pursue this opportunity. Your help means so much to me.

Finally, thank you to my editor, Scott Nybakken, for guiding me through the cookbook process and helping to bring these anime pastries to life!

TITAN
BOOKS

144 Southwark Street
London SE1 OUP

www.titanbooks.com

Find us on Facebook: www.facebook.com/titanbooks

Follow us on Twitter: @titanbooks

A CIP catalogue record for this title is available from the British Library.

ISBN: 978-1-80336-107-9

Publisher: Raoul Goff
VP of Licensing and Partnerships: Vanessa Lopez
VP of Creative: Chrissy Kwasnik
VP of Manufacturing: Alix Nicholaeff
Editorial Director: Vicki Jaeger
Designer: Monique Narboneta Zosa
Editor: Scott Nybakken
Editorial Assistant: Harrison Tunggal
Senior Production Editor: Elaine Ou
Production Manager: Sam Taylor
Senior Production Manager, Subsidiary Rights: Lina s Palma

Photographer: Emily Hawkes
Food Stylist: Hadley Sui
Prop Stylist: Andrea Greco
Photo Assistant: Regina Tamburro
Photo Intern: Shelby Antel
Food Styling Assistants: Sarah Pleitez & Debbie Wee
Shooting location: Dutchess Studios, Long Island City

ROOTS of PEACE   REPLANTED PAPER

Insight Editions, in association with Roots of Peace, will plant
two trees for each tree used in the manufacturing of this book.
Roots of Peace is an internationally renowned humanitarian
organization dedicated to eradicating land mines worldwide and
converting war-torn lands into productive farms and wildlife
habitats. Roots of Peace will plant two million fruit and nut
trees in Afghanistan and provide farmers there with the skills
and support necessary for sustainable land use.

Manufactured in China by Insight Editions

10 9 8 7 6 5 4 3 2 1